Beyond CRUD: Advanced Django Techniques for Next-Level Web Applications

ISBN:

Published by: **Ekesy In-Outdoor Company**

10B, Mufutau Opeifa Street, Oke-Odo, Ile-Epo B/Stop, Alimosho, Lagos, Nigeria

Email: care@israeljoshua.com.ng

Tel: +234 803 815 4459, +234 813 2228 534

Printed by: **Demrok Prints**

For information, please contact us @

care@israeljoshua.com.ng

israeljoshua.com.ng

Call: +234 803 815 4459

Whatsapp: +234 813 2228 534

Table of Content

Dedication

To the Almighty God

In humble gratitude, I dedicate this book to the Almighty God, the source of wisdom, inspiration, and guidance throughout the journey of crafting these advanced Django techniques. His unwavering support has illuminated the path and fueled the passion for sharing knowledge in the ever-evolving realm of web development.

To My Precious Kids

To my beloved children, you are the heartbeat that propels me forward. Your joy, curiosity, and boundless energy have been a constant reminder of the importance of continuous learning and growth. This book stands as a testament to the legacy we strive to build, shaping a future where knowledge is treasured and shared.

To My Cherished Mum

To my dear mother, your sacrifices, encouragement, and enduring love have been the pillars that sustained me. This book is a tribute to your unwavering belief in the power of education and the pursuit of dreams. Your resilience and strength are woven into these pages.

To My Esteemed Readers

To you, my esteemed readers, this dedication extends to express deep gratitude. Your curiosity, enthusiasm, and commitment to advancing your skills inspire the creation of content that transcends the ordinary. May this book serve as a valuable companion on your journey to mastering advanced Django techniques.

In the spirit of continuous improvement and shared knowledge, let us embark on this exploration of "Beyond CRUD: Advanced Django Techniques for Next-Level Web Applications." May it empower you to elevate your web development endeavors and contribute to the broader community.

With gratitude and warm regards,

Israel Joshua Chukwubueze

Preface

In the ever-evolving landscape of web development, mastering Django goes beyond the basics of Create, Read, Update, and Delete (CRUD) operations. As technology advances and user expectations soar, the need for next-level web applications becomes increasingly apparent. It is within this context that "Beyond CRUD: Advanced Django Techniques for Next-Level Web Applications" emerges.

My Transformation

Formerly known as Christopher Ekene Okade, I embarked on a transformative journey fueled by my unwavering passion for writing and sharing knowledge. This journey led me to adopt the name Israel Joshua Chukwubueze, symbolizing a new chapter of growth, purpose, and authenticity. With a renewed sense of identity and purpose, I embarked on the creation of this book, driven by the desire to equip aspiring developers and seasoned professionals alike with the tools and techniques needed to excel in Django development.

A Passion for Sharing

At the heart of this endeavor lies a deep-seated passion for sharing knowledge. Throughout my career in software development, I have witnessed the transformative power of education and mentorship. From my early days as a novice programmer to my current role as an experienced developer, I have been fortunate to learn from mentors who generously shared their expertise and insights. It is this ethos of generosity and collaboration that motivates me to pay it forward through the pages of this book.

Unveiling Advanced Techniques

"Beyond CRUD" is more than just a technical manual; it is a comprehensive guide to unlocking the full potential of Django for building sophisticated web applications. Each chapter delves into advanced techniques and best practices, offering practical insights, real-world examples, and actionable tips for elevating your Django projects to new heights. Whether you're seeking to optimize performance, integrate cutting-edge technologies, or navigate the complexities of microservices architecture, this book serves as your indispensable companion.

A Journey of Discovery

As you embark on this journey through "Beyond CRUD," I encourage you to approach each topic with curiosity and enthusiasm. Embrace the challenges, celebrate the victories, and cherish the moments of discovery along the way. Remember that mastery is not achieved overnight but through persistence, practice, and a willingness to embrace lifelong learning.

Gratitude and Acknowledgments

I extend my heartfelt gratitude to all those who have supported me on this journey – from mentors and colleagues to friends and family. Your encouragement, feedback, and unwavering belief in my abilities have been instrumental in bringing this book to fruition. Special thanks to the readers whose curiosity and thirst for knowledge inspire me to continue pushing the boundaries of what is possible in the world of Django development.

Embark on the Journey

Now, without further ado, I invite you to immerse yourself in the world of "Beyond CRUD." Let us embark together on a journey of exploration, growth, and discovery as we uncover the advanced Django techniques that will propel your web applications to the next level.

With warm regards,

Israel Joshua Chukwubueze

About the Author:
Israel Joshua Chukwubueze

The Author's Official Website
Learn more about the Passion, Talents and Skills

Click here to:
https://israeljoshua.com.ng/

I know you will Enjoy this Book and don't forget to leave a review for this book.
Click Here to Leave a Review!

Chapter 1: Introduction to Advanced Django Concepts

Django, a high-level Python web framework, has evolved significantly since its inception. In this chapter, we'll trace the evolution of Django, emphasizing its historical context, major releases, and updates. We'll then delve into the importance of moving beyond CRUD operations, exploring the limitations of CRUD and understanding real-world scenarios that demand increased complexity. Finally, we'll guide you through setting up the project environment, covering virtual environments, dependencies, and best practices in project structure.

1.1 Overview of Django's Evolution

Django's journey is marked by continuous improvement, innovation, and community contributions. Understanding its evolution is crucial for appreciating the advanced concepts introduced in this book.

1.1.1 Historical Context

Django originated in the newsroom of the Lawrence Journal-World newspaper in 2003, developed by Adrian Holovaty and Simon Willison. Its primary goal was to simplify the web development process, emphasizing DRY (Don't Repeat Yourself) principles. Over the years, Django has become an open-source project maintained by the Django Software Foundation.

Django, an open-source web framework written in Python, was first developed in 2003 by Adrian Holovaty and Simon Willison. Initially, it was an in-house project for the Lawrence Journal-World newspaper to handle content management for their online publications. Later, in 2005, it was released under a BSD license, making it accessible to the public. Since its inception, Django has gained popularity and is currently maintained by the Django Software Foundation, which was founded in 2008.

The primary motivation behind Django's creation was the need for a rapid development framework that adheres to the DRY (Don't Repeat Yourself) principle. This principle encourages developers to minimize redundancy in their code by reusing components, leading to increased productivity, maintainability, and code consistency.

1.1.2 Major Releases and Updates

Django's major releases, such as 1.0, 1.5, 2.0, and subsequent updates, brought significant enhancements. Each release introduced new features, improved security, and addressed community feedback. Notable updates include the introduction of the Django Admin interface, support for class-based views, and the adoption of Python 3.

Throughout its evolution, Django has seen numerous updates and releases, each introducing new features, improvements, and bug fixes. Some of the major releases include:

1. Django 1.0 (2008): Introduced the ORM (Object-Relational Mapping) system, simplifying database interaction, and the admin interface, enhancing the backend management experience.
2. Django 1.2 (2010): Introduced class-based views, improving the organization and readability of view code.
3. Django 1.6 (2014): Introduced the new forms system, improving the way developers create and handle form submissions.
4. Django 1.8 (2015): Introduced migrations, allowing developers to manage database schema changes more efficiently.
5. Django 2.0 (2017): Dropped support for Python 2 and introduced the new URL routing system, improving the way developers define application routes.
6. Django 3.0 (2019): Introduced the new `AppConfig` system, allowing more fine-grained control over application configuration.

1.2 Importance of Advancing Beyond CRUD

CRUD (Create, Read, Update, Delete) operations form the foundation of many web applications. However, to tackle real-world challenges, developers must move beyond CRUD and embrace advanced Django concepts.

1.2.1 The Limitations of CRUD

While CRUD provides a straightforward way to interact with databases, it falls short when dealing with complex business logic and intricate data relationships. Advanced Django techniques empower developers to handle more sophisticated scenarios, such as hierarchical data structures and intricate data validations.

CRUD (Create, Read, Update, Delete) is a common acronym used to describe the fundamental building blocks of data manipulation in web applications. While CRUD operations are essential for basic data management, they often fail to address real-world scenarios requiring more complex functionality.

CRUD applications typically focus on data input, retrieval, modification, and deletion, often neglecting essential features such as user authentication, authorization, content management, and external service integration. As a result, developers often find themselves limited by the constraints of CRUD applications, leading to the need for more advanced concepts in Django.

1.2.2 Real-World Scenarios Demanding Complexity

Consider an e-commerce platform with multiple roles, including customers, sellers, and administrators. Implementing features like inventory management, order processing, and real-time notifications requires a more nuanced approach than traditional CRUD operations. Advanced Django concepts enable developers to architect solutions that meet these challenges head-on.

In real-world scenarios, web applications often require more than just CRUD operations. Some examples include:

1. User authentication and authorization: Implementing user registration, login, and permission management to ensure secure access to specific resources.
2. Content management: Developing custom content management systems, allowing users to create, modify, and delete content in a structured and organized manner.
3. External service integration: Integrating third-party services, such as payment gateways and social media platforms, to extend application functionality and reach.
4. Performance optimization: Implementing caching mechanisms and load balancing techniques to ensure applications can handle high traffic and large datasets.
5. Scalability: Designing and implementing applications that can grow and adapt to changing requirements, such as expanding to accommodate additional users or resources.

1.3 Setting Up the Project Environment

Before diving into advanced Django concepts, it's crucial to establish a robust project environment. This involves creating a virtual environment, managing dependencies, and adhering to best practices in project structure.

1.3.1 Virtual Environments and Dependencies

Virtual environments are a crucial aspect of managing dependencies and ensuring a consistent development environment across different projects. A virtual environment is a self-contained Python environment that allows developers to install and manage project-specific dependencies without affecting the global Python installation.

A virtual environment isolates project dependencies, preventing conflicts with other projects. Create a virtual environment using `venv` or `virtualenv`:

```
##(CMD/Terminal)
python -m venv myenv
```
Activate the virtual environment:

- On Windows: `myenv\Scripts\activate`
- On Unix or MacOS: `source myenv/bin/activate`

Install project dependencies:

```
##(CMD/Terminal)
pip install -r requirements.txt
```

1.3.2 Best Practices in Project Structure

When structuring Django projects, adhering to best practices can lead to more maintainable and scalable applications. Here are some recommended practices for project structure:

1. Separate settings: Organize settings files by environment (development, staging, production) and use environment variables to avoid hardcoding sensitive information.
2. Applications: Organize applications by functionality and adhere to the single responsibility principle, ensuring each application handles a specific task.
3. Templates: Use a consistent template structure and follow the DRY principle by creating reusable template components, such as base templates and template tags.
4. Static files: Organize static files (CSS, JavaScript, images) by type and application and use a consistent naming convention.
5. Tests: Create a separate directory for tests and follow a consistent naming convention for test files, such as `test_*.py`.

Organizing your Django project effectively enhances maintainability. Adopt a structure that separates concerns and follows Django's recommended layout:

- **project/**
  - **app/**

- ■ __init__.py
  - ■ admin.py
  - ■ apps.py
  - ■ migrations/
  - ■ models.py
  - ■ tests/
  - ■ views.py
- ○ manage.py
- ○ requirements.txt
- ○ settings.py
- ○ urls.py
- ○ wsgi.py

Example Codes:

```python
# Example Code 1: Creating a Virtual
Environment
python -m venv myenv


# Example Code 2: Activating the Virtual
Environment (Windows)
myenv\Scripts\activate


# Example Code 3: Installing
Dependencies from requirements.txt
pip install -r requirements.txt
```

Tips:

1. **Isolation is Key:** Always use virtual environments to isolate project dependencies. This avoids conflicts and ensures a clean environment for your Django project.

2. **Keep It DRY:** Adhere to the DRY principle in project structure. Reusable apps, modular components, and separation of concerns contribute to a cleaner and more maintainable codebase.

3. **Document Your Dependencies:** Maintain a clear `requirements.txt` file listing all project dependencies. This ensures consistent environments for development, testing, and deployment.

4. **Version Control Your Environment:** Include your virtual environment in version control to replicate the exact environment across different development machines.

5. **Follow Django Conventions:** Stick to Django's project structure conventions to make your project more accessible to other developers and adhere to best practices.

Examples Tips

1. Use a linter: Adopting a linter, such as Flake8 or Pylint, can help enforce consistent code style and catch potential issues before they become problems.
2. Use version control: Integrating version control, such

as Git, into your Django projects can help track changes, facilitate collaboration, and version application releases.
3. Leverage pre-built packages: Utilize pre-built packages, such as Django Rest Framework for API development and Django CMS for content management, to accelerate development and reduce the need for custom solutions.

In conclusion, understanding the evolution of Django, the limitations of CRUD, and best practices for project structure is essential for advanced Django development. Adopting these principles can lead to more maintainable, scalable, and secure applications, ensuring a positive experience for both developers and end-users.

In this chapter, we've laid the groundwork by exploring the evolution of Django, recognizing the need to move beyond CRUD operations, and establishing a solid project environment. Armed with this knowledge, you're ready to delve into the advanced Django techniques covered in the subsequent chapters.

Chapter 2: Going Beyond Models and Views

In this chapter, we'll dive into advanced Django concepts that extend beyond the basic foundations of models and views. We'll explore advanced model relationships, custom managers and querysets, and the power of class-based views and mixins.

2.1 Advanced Model Relationships

Django's ORM provides a powerful way to model database relationships. Going beyond the basics, let's explore one-to-one relationships, many-to-many relationships, and the use of custom through models.

2.1.1 One-to-One Relationships

One-to-one relationships are useful when you want to associate exactly one related model with another. This is achieved by using the `OneToOneField`. For example, consider a scenario where each user has exactly one profile:

```python
# Example Code 1: One-to-One
Relationship
from django.db import models

class UserProfile(models.Model):
    user = models.OneToOneField(User,
on_delete=models.CASCADE)
```

```python
    bio = models.TextField()
    # other fields...

# Tip 1: One-to-One Relationship
# Use OneToOneField when you have a
unique relationship between two models,
like a user profile.
```

This field type ensures that a single instance of one model is associated with a single instance of another model. For example, consider a `User` model and a `Profile` model, where each user has a single profile.

python
```python
class Profile(models.Model):
    user = models.OneToOneField(User,
on_delete=models.CASCADE)
    # Additional fields for the profile
```

When using one-to-one relationships, it is essential to consider the following:

1. Use the `on_delete` parameter to specify how Django should handle the deletion of related objects.
2. Use the `related_name` parameter to specify a custom name for the reverse relationship.

2.1.2 Many-to-Many Relationships

Many-to-many relationships are common in scenarios where each instance of one model can be associated with multiple instances of another model. The `ManyToManyField` facilitates this relationship:

```python
# Example Code 2: Many-to-Many
Relationship
from django.db import models

class Movie(models.Model):
    title =
models.CharField(max_length=255)
    actors =
models.ManyToManyField(Actor)
    # other fields...

# Tip 2: Many-to-Many Relationship
# Use ManyToManyField when multiple
instances of one model can be associated
with multiple instances of another
model.
```

This field type allows multiple instances of one model to be associated with multiple instances of another model. For example, consider a `Book` model and an `Author` model, where multiple authors can write multiple books.

```python
class Book(models.Model):
    authors =
```

```
models.ManyToManyField(Author)
```

When using many-to-many relationships, it is essential to consider the following:

1. Use the `through` parameter to specify a custom intermediary model when additional fields are required for the relationship.
2. Use the `symmetrical` parameter to specify whether the relationship should be symmetrical.

2.1.3 Custom Through Models

When you need additional fields on a many-to-many relationship, Django allows you to use a custom through model. This model represents the intermediate table between the two related models:

```python
# Example Code 3: Custom Through Model
from django.db import models

class MovieRole(models.Model):
    movie = models.ForeignKey(Movie,
on_delete=models.CASCADE)
    actor = models.ForeignKey(Actor,
on_delete=models.CASCADE)
    role =
models.CharField(max_length=255)
    # other fields...

# Tip 3: Custom Through Model
```

Use a custom through model when you need to store additional information about the relationship between two models in a many-to-many relationship.

Custom through models are used when additional fields are required for many-to-many relationships. For example, consider a `Membership` model that represents a many-to-many relationship between `User` and `Group`, but also includes the `join_date` and `expiration_date` fields.

python
```python
class Membership(models.Model):
    user = models.ForeignKey(User,
on_delete=models.CASCADE)
    group = models.ForeignKey(Group,
on_delete=models.CASCADE)
    join_date =
models.DateTimeField(auto_now_add=True)
    expiration_date =
models.DateTimeField()

class Group(models.Model):
    name =
models.CharField(max_length=100)
    members =
models.ManyToManyField(User,
through=Membership)
```

2.2 Custom Managers and QuerySets

Django Managers and QuerySets allow for flexible data retrieval and manipulation. Let's explore writing custom querysets and extending managers to enhance the capabilities of your models.

2.2.1 Writing Custom QuerySets

Custom querysets enable you to define reusable query logic for your models. For example, creating a custom queryset to retrieve all active users:

```python
# Example Code 4: Custom QuerySet
from django.db import models

class UserManager(models.Manager):
    def get_queryset(self):
        return super().get_queryset().filter(is_active=True)

class User(models.Model):
    # fields...
    objects = UserManager()


# Tip 4: Custom QuerySet
# Utilize custom querysets to encapsulate complex or frequently used queries for your models.
```

Custom QuerySets allow developers to create custom methods for querying and filtering data within the database. For example, consider a `BlogPost` model with a custom `popular_posts` QuerySet method.

python
```python
class BlogPostQuerySet(models.QuerySet):
    def popular_posts(self):
        return
self.filter(views__gte=1000)

class BlogPost(models.Model):
    title =
models.CharField(max_length=100)
    content = models.TextField()
    views =
models.IntegerField(default=0)

    objects =
BlogPostQuerySet.as_manager()
```

2.2.2 Extending Django Managers

Django managers allow you to encapsulate model-level logic. Extending managers can help you create reusable functionality accessible through your models:

python
```python
# Example Code 5: Extending Django
```

```python
Manager
from django.db import models

class PublishedManager(models.Manager):
    def get_queryset(self):
        return
super().get_queryset().filter(status='pu
blished')

class Article(models.Model):
    # fields...
    status =
models.CharField(max_length=10,
choices=[('draft', 'Draft'),
('published', 'Published')])
    objects = models.Manager()  #
Default manager
    published_objects =
PublishedManager()  # Custom manager for
published articles

# Tip 5: Extending Django Manager
# Extend managers to encapsulate common
query patterns and keep your model's
logic organized.
```

Custom managers can be used to extend Django's built-in managers, providing additional functionality for querying and filtering data within the database. For example, consider a `Book` model with a custom `published` manager that only returns published books.

python
```python
class PublishedManager(models.Manager):
    def get_queryset(self):
        return
super().get_queryset().filter(status='p'
)

class Book(models.Model):
    title =
models.CharField(max_length=100)
    content = models.TextField()
    status =
models.CharField(max_length=10,
choices=(('p', 'Published'), ('d',
'Draft')))

    published = PublishedManager()
    all_books = models.Manager()
```

2.3 Class-Based Views and Mixins

Class-based views provide a more structured way to
organize your view logic. Understanding class-based views
and creating custom mixins can lead to more maintainable
and modular code.

2.3.1 Understanding Class-Based Views

Class-based views (CBVs) are a powerful way to organize
view logic using Python classes. They offer better code

organization and reusability compared to function-based views. CBVs are based on the class inheritance model, where a base class provides common functionality, and subclasses can extend or override that functionality.

Examples of CBVs include the `ListView`, `DetailView`, `CreateView`, and `UpdateView`. These views provide a simple and standardized way to handle common use cases, such as displaying a list of objects or creating a new object.
Here's an example:

```python
# Example Code 6: Class-Based View

from django.views import View
from django.http import HttpResponse

class HelloWorldView(View):
    def get(self, request):
        return HttpResponse("Hello, World!")

# Tip 6: Class-Based View
# Use class-based views for better
organization, especially when dealing
with complex views that require multiple
HTTP methods.
```

2.3.2 Creating Custom Mixins

Mixins are reusable pieces of code that can be combined with class-based views to add functionality. For example, creating a mixin for adding authentication to a view:

```python
# Example Code 7: Custom Mixin

from django.contrib.auth.decorators import login_required
from django.utils.decorators import method_decorator

class LoginRequiredMixin:
    @method_decorator(login_required)
    def dispatch(self, *args, **kwargs):
        return super().dispatch(*args, **kwargs)

# Tip 7: Custom Mixin
# Use mixins to encapsulate reusable functionality and easily combine them with your class-based views.
```

Mixins allow developers to add custom behavior to views without the need for multiple inheritance.

For example, consider a custom mixin that adds pagination functionality to any class-based view.

```python
class PaginationMixin:
```

```python
    def get_paginate_by(self, queryset):
        if self.request.is_ajax():
            return self.paginate_by_ajax
        return self.paginate_by

    def get_context_data(self,
**kwargs):
        context =
super().get_context_data(**kwargs)
        if self.request.is_ajax():
            context['page_obj'] =
context['object_list']
            context['is_paginated'] =
False
            context['paginator'] = None
        return context

    def paginate_queryset(self,
queryset, page_size):
        if self.request.is_ajax():
            paginator =
PaginatorAjax(queryset, page_size)
            return
paginator.get_page(self.request.GET.get(
'page'))
        return
super().paginate_queryset(queryset,
page_size)
```

Examples and Tips

1. Use custom managers to enforce constraints: Custom managers can be used to enforce constraints on the data within the database, ensuring data integrity and consistency.
2. Leverage mixins for reusability: Mixins allow developers to create reusable components that can be used across multiple views, reducing code duplication and improving maintainability.
3. Understand the lifecycle of CBVs: Understanding the lifecycle of class-based views, such as the order in which methods are called, is essential for customizing and extending their functionality.

In conclusion, understanding advanced model relationships, custom managers and querysets, and class-based views and mixins is essential for advanced Django development. Adopting these principles can lead to more maintainable, scalable, and efficient applications, ensuring a positive experience for both developers and end-users.

In this chapter, we've explored advanced model relationships, custom managers and querysets, and the power of class-based views and mixins. These concepts form the basis for building sophisticated and maintainable Django applications. As you progress through this book, these foundational elements will become crucial for implementing advanced web application features.

Chapter 3: Mastering Django Forms

Forms are a critical component in web development, serving as the bridge between the user and the application. In this chapter, we'll dive into mastering Django forms by exploring advanced concepts such as formsets, custom form validation, and Django form widgets.

3.1 Formsets and Inline Formsets

Django provides formsets to manage multiple forms on a single page efficiently. Formsets are useful when dealing with scenarios where users need to submit or interact with multiple instances of a form. Let's explore handling multiple forms on one page and dynamically adding and removing forms.

3.1.1 Handling Multiple Forms on One Page

Formsets simplify the process of managing multiple forms on a single page. For example, assume you have a scenario where a user can submit multiple comments on a blog post:

```python
# Example Code 1: Formsets
from django import forms
from django.forms import formset_factory

class CommentForm(forms.Form):
    text = forms.CharField()
```

```python
CommentFormSet =
formset_factory(CommentForm, extra=2,
max_num=10)

# Tip 1: Formsets
# Use formsets when dealing with
scenarios where users need to interact
with or submit multiple instances of a
form on a single page.
```

Formsets provide a way to handle multiple forms on a single page in Django. This capability is useful when dealing with collections of data, such as creating or editing multiple records at once.

To create a formset, use the `formset_factory` function, passing in the desired form class and an additional `extra` parameter to specify the number of additional forms to include.

python
```python
from django.forms import formset_factory
from .forms import MyForm


MyFormSet = formset_factory(MyForm,
extra=3)
```
Formsets also include a `management_form` that should be rendered alongside the formset to ensure proper handling of the forms.

3.1.2 Dynamically Adding and Removing Forms

In certain situations, dynamically adding and removing forms can enhance the user experience. JavaScript can be employed to achieve this dynamic behavior:

```python
# Example Code 2: Dynamically Adding and
Removing Forms
# HTML and JavaScript code to
dynamically manage formsets on the
client side.


# Tip 2: Dynamically Adding and Removing
Forms
# Employ JavaScript libraries like
jQuery or native JavaScript to
dynamically manage and manipulate
formsets on the client side.
```

Django provides the `formset_factory` function with the `can_delete` and `can_order` parameters, enabling dynamic addition and removal of forms.

For dynamically adding forms, use the `formset_factory` function with the `can_delete` parameter set to `True`.

```python
```

```python
MyFormSet = formset_factory(MyForm,
can_delete=True)
```

For dynamically removing forms, use the `ManagementForm` and `formset.delete()` methods.

html

```html
<form method="post">
    {% csrf_token %}
    {{ formset.management_form }}
    {% for form in formset %}
        {{ form.as_p }}
        <input type="submit"
name="delete_{{ forloop.parentloop.count
er }}" value="Delete">
    {% endfor %}
</form>
```

python

```python
if 'delete_1' in request.POST:
    formset.delete(0)
```

3.2 Custom Form Validation

Django forms come with built-in validation, but in advanced scenarios, you may need to override default validation methods or create custom validators.

3.2.1 Overriding Form Validation Methods

When the default form validation is not sufficient, you can override methods like `clean()` to implement custom validation logic:

```python
# Example Code 3: Overriding Form
Validation Methods
from django import forms


class CustomForm(forms.Form):
    def clean(self):
        cleaned_data = super().clean()
        # Custom validation logic here
```

Custom form validation can be achieved by overriding the `clean` and `clean_<field_name>` methods in a form class. The `clean` method is used to perform cross-field validation, while the `clean_<field_name>` method is used to perform field-specific validation.

```python
class MyForm(forms.Form):
    username = forms.CharField()
    password = forms.CharField()

    def clean_username(self):
        username = self.cleaned_data['username']
        if User.objects.filter(username=username).exists():
            raise forms.ValidationError('Username already
```

```python
exists')
        return username

    def clean(self):
        username =
self.cleaned_data['username']
        password =
self.cleaned_data['password']
        if len(password) < 8:
            self.add_error('password',
'Password must be at least 8
characters')
```

3.2.2 Creating Custom Validators

For more granular validation, Django allows you to create
custom validators. These validators can be applied to
individual fields:

```python
python
# Example Code 4: Custom Validators
from django.core.exceptions import
ValidationError
from django.utils.translation import
gettext_lazy as _

def validate_even(value):
    if value % 2 != 0:
        raise ValidationError(
            _('Value must be an even
number'),
```

```python
        params={'value': value},
    )
```

```python
# Tip 3: Overriding Form Validation Methods
# Override form validation methods like clean() when you need to perform complex validation that involves multiple fields.
```

```python
# Tip 4: Creating Custom Validators
# Create custom validators for specific fields to enforce business rules and ensure data integrity.
```

Custom validators can be created and reused across multiple forms and fields. To create a custom validator, define a function that accepts a single parameter and raises a ValidationError exception if the validation fails.

python
```python
from django.core.exceptions import ValidationError


def validate_positive_integer(value):
    if value <= 0:
        raise ValidationError('Value must be a positive integer')

class MyForm(forms.Form):
```

```python
    number = forms.IntegerField(validators=[validate_positive_integer])
```

3.3 Django Form Widgets

Form widgets define how data is presented and accepted in a form field. Django provides various built-in widgets, and you can create custom widgets to tailor the form's appearance.

3.3.1 Exploring Built-in Widgets

Django comes with a range of built-in widgets catering to different data types. For instance, the `DateInput` widget for handling date input:

```python
# Example Code 5: Exploring Built-in Widgets
from django import forms

class DateForm(forms.Form):
    date_field = forms.DateField(widget=forms.DateInput(attrs={'type': 'date'}))


# Tip 5: Exploring Built-in Widgets
# Familiarize yourself with Django's built-in widgets to efficiently handle various types of form data.
```

Django provides several built-in widgets, such as
`TextInput`, `Select`, `CheckboxInput`, and
`DateInput`, to handle various types of form inputs.

python
```python
class MyForm(forms.Form):
    name =
forms.CharField(widget=forms.TextInput(a
ttrs={'class': 'form-control'}))
    age =
forms.IntegerField(widget=forms.NumberIn
put(attrs={'class': 'form-control'}))
    gender =
forms.ChoiceField(choices=[('M',
'Male'), ('F', 'Female')],
widget=forms.RadioSelect())
```

3.3.2 Creating Custom Widgets

When the built-in widgets don't meet your specific
requirements, you can create custom widgets:

python
```python
# Example Code 6: Creating Custom
Widgets
from django import forms

class CustomTextarea(forms.Textarea):
    def __init__(self, attrs=None):
        default_attrs = {'class':
'custom-textarea'}
```

```python
        if attrs:
            default_attrs.update(attrs)
        super().__init__(default_attrs)
```

Tip 6: Creating Custom Widgets
Craft custom widgets when you need specialized input or display elements in your forms.

Custom widgets can be created by subclassing the `Widget` class and overriding the `render` method.

python
```python
class MyWidget(widgets.Widget):
    def render(self, name, value, attrs=None):
        return mark_safe(f'<div id="{name}">{value}</div>')

class MyForm(forms.Form):
    message = forms.CharField(widget=MyWidget())
```

Examples and Tips

1. Use formsets for handling multiple forms: Formsets provide a convenient way to handle multiple forms on a single page, simplifying the process of editing and creating collections of data.
2. Leverage custom validation methods: Custom form

validation is a powerful tool for ensuring data integrity and consistency, enabling developers to enforce business rules and constraints.

3. Utilize built-in widgets: Built-in widgets provide a wide range of functionality for handling various types of form inputs, reducing the need for custom solutions.

4. Create custom widgets for unique use cases: Custom widgets allow developers to create unique and specialized form inputs for specific use cases, enhancing the user experience and improving data input.

In conclusion, mastering Django forms is essential for advanced Django development. Adopting these principles can lead to more maintainable, scalable, and user-friendly applications, ensuring a positive experience for both developers and end-users.

In this chapter, we've delved into advanced Django form concepts, including the use of formsets for managing multiple forms on a page, custom form validation techniques, and the exploration of built-in and custom form widgets. Armed with these advanced form-handling skills, you'll be well-equipped to build robust and user-friendly web applications using Django.

Chapter 4: Advanced Django Admin

Django's admin interface is a powerful tool for managing data in your application. In this chapter, we'll explore advanced techniques to customize the Django admin interface, add custom actions, and implement security measures to protect sensitive data.

4.1 Customizing the Django Admin Interface

4.1.1 Admin Styling and Theming

The appearance of the Django admin interface can be customized to align with the branding of your application or to provide a more user-friendly experience. Customizing styles and themes can be achieved by overriding the default CSS styles.

Example Code 1: Admin Styling and Theming

```python
python
# admin.py
from django.contrib import admin

class CustomAdminSite(admin.AdminSite):
    # Custom CSS styles
    custom_styles = {
        'base.css': 'custom/base.css',
    }

    # Override method to add custom
styles
```

```python
    def each_context(self, request):
        context = super().each_context(request)
        context['custom_styles'] = self.custom_styles
        return context


# Register your models with the custom admin site
admin_site = CustomAdminSite(name='customadmin')
```

Django's built-in admin interface is functional but lacks visual appeal. To enhance the appearance of the admin interface, developers can use third-party packages such as `django-admin-bootstrap` and `django-admin-reorder`. These packages allow for customization of the admin interface's layout, styling, and branding.

Another option is to utilize custom CSS and JavaScript to style the admin interface. To add custom CSS and JavaScript, create a file in the project's templates directory and include it in the admin's base template.

html
```html
{% block extrahead %}
    <link rel="stylesheet" type="text/css" href="{% static 'path/to/admin.css' %}">
    <script type="text/javascript" src="{% static 'path/to/admin.js' %}"></
```

```
script>
{% endblock %}
```

Tip 1: Admin Styling and Theming

- Customize the Django admin interface to match your application's design and branding.
- Be mindful of user experience when applying styling changes.

4.1.2 Customizing List Views and Detail Views

Django admin allows customization of list views and detail views to display additional information or actions related to your models.

Example Code 2: Customizing List Views and Detail Views

```python
# admin.py
from django.contrib import admin

class CustomModelAdmin(admin.ModelAdmin):
    list_display = ('name', 'description', 'custom_method')

    def custom_method(self, obj):
        return f"{obj.name} -
```

```python
{obj.description}"

    custom_method.short_description =
'Custom Method'
```

Tip 2: Customizing List Views and Detail Views

- Use `list_display` to specify fields or methods to be displayed in the list view.
- Leverage methods within the model admin class for custom logic or display.

4.1.2 Customizing List Views and Detail Views

Customizing list views and detail views in Django's admin interface can be achieved by creating custom `ModelAdmin` classes for each model. These classes can override various methods to customize the display and behavior of the admin interface.

For example, to customize the list view, override the `list_display` attribute.

python
```python
class MyModelAdmin(admin.ModelAdmin):
    list_display = ('name', 'created_at')

admin.site.register(MyModel, MyModelAdmin)
```
To customize the detail view, override the

`change_form_template` attribute.

```python
class MyModelAdmin(admin.ModelAdmin):
    change_form_template = 'path/to/custom_change_form.html'

admin.site.register(MyModel, MyModelAdmin)
```

4.2 Adding Actions to Django Admin

4.2.1 Writing Custom Admin Actions

Admin actions allow you to perform bulk operations on selected objects in the Django admin interface. Custom actions can be added to provide specific functionalities tailored to your application.

Example Code 3: Writing Custom Admin Actions

```python
# admin.py
from django.contrib import admin

class CustomModelAdmin(admin.ModelAdmin):
    actions = ['custom_action']

    def custom_action(self, request, queryset):
```

```python
        # Custom logic for the action
        queryset.update(status='approved')

    custom_action.short_description = 'Approve selected items'
```

Tip 3: Writing Custom Admin Actions

- Utilize admin actions to perform bulk operations on selected objects.
- Provide a meaningful description for custom actions to enhance user understanding.

Custom admin actions can be added to Django's admin interface to perform custom operations on selected objects. To create a custom admin action, define a function in a `ModelAdmin` class that accepts a request object and a queryset.

python
```python
class MyModelAdmin(admin.ModelAdmin):
    actions = ['my_custom_action']

    def my_custom_action(self, request, queryset):
        # Perform custom operation
        pass

admin.site.register(MyModel, MyModelAdmin)
```

4.2.2 Bulk Actions and Confirmations

When implementing custom actions, it's essential to consider user experience and confirmations to prevent unintended changes.

Example Code 4: Bulk Actions and Confirmations

```python
# admin.py
from django.contrib import admin

class CustomModelAdmin(admin.ModelAdmin):
    actions = ['custom_action']

    def custom_action(self, request, queryset):
        # Custom logic for the action

queryset.update(status='approved')

    custom_action.short_description = 'Approve selected items'
    actions_on_top = True
    actions_on_bottom = True
    actions_selection_counter = True
```

Tip 4: Bulk Actions and Confirmations

- Set `actions_on_top` and `actions_on_bottom` to `True` to display action buttons at the top and bottom of the change list page.
- Enable `actions_selection_counter` to show the number of selected items for better user feedback.

Bulk actions in Django's admin interface allow users to perform actions on multiple objects simultaneously. To enable bulk actions, define a function in a `ModelAdmin` class that accepts a request object and a queryset.

python
```python
class MyModelAdmin(admin.ModelAdmin):
    actions = ['my_bulk_action']

    def my_bulk_action(self, request, queryset):
        # Perform custom operation
        pass

admin.site.register(MyModel, MyModelAdmin)
```
To add a confirmation step to a bulk action, return a `HttpResponse` object with a redirect to the admin's change list page with a `post` parameter.

python
```python
from django.http import HttpResponseRedirect
```

```python
class MyModelAdmin(admin.ModelAdmin):
    actions = ['my_bulk_action']


    def my_bulk_action(self, request,
queryset):
        # Perform custom operation
        if request.POST.get('post'):
            # Perform bulk operation
            return
HttpResponseRedirect('../')
        else:
            confirmation_message = 'Are
you sure you want to perform this action
on the selected objects?'
            return
HttpResponseRedirect('../../?
post=yes&%s' %
self.admin_site.build_query_string(confi
rm=confirmation_message))


admin.site.register(MyModel,
MyModelAdmin)
```

4.3 Security Considerations in Django Admin

4.3.1 Limiting Access with Permissions

Django admin provides a robust permissions system that
allows fine-grained control over user access. Assigning
appropriate permissions ensures that users have access only

to the necessary admin functionalities.

Example Code 5: Limiting Access with Permissions

```python
python
# admin.py
from django.contrib import admin

class CustomModelAdmin(admin.ModelAdmin):
    # Restrict access to specific actions
    actions = ['custom_action']
    required_permission = 'myapp.can_custom_action'

    def has_change_permission(self, request, obj=None):
        # Check for the required permission
        if request.user.has_perm(self.required_permission):
            return True
        return False
```

Tip 5: Limiting Access with Permissions

- Use the `has_change_permission` method to customize access based on user permissions.
- Assign permissions at a granular level to control

access to specific actions.

Django's built-in permission system can be used to limit access to the admin interface and specific models. To assign permissions to users, use Django's built-in permission management interface or create custom permission management views.

python
```python
from django.contrib.auth.models import Permission
from django.shortcuts import import render


def assign_permissions(request):
    if request.method == 'POST':
        user = User.objects.get(id=request.POST['user_id'])
        model = ContentType.objects.get(app_label='myapp', model='mymodel')
        permission = Permission.objects.get(codename='view_mymodel')
        user.user_permissions.add(permission)
        return HttpResponseRedirect('/admin/')
    else:
        users = User.objects.all()
```

```python
        return render(request, 'path/to/
assign_permissions.html', {'users':
users})
```

4.3.2 Implementing Two-Factor Authentication

Enhancing the security of the Django admin interface can involve implementing additional layers of authentication, such as two-factor authentication (2FA).

Example Code 6: Implementing Two-Factor Authentication

```python
python
# settings.py
INSTALLED_APPS = [
    # ...
    'django_otp',
    'django_otp.plugins.otp_totp',
    'django.contrib.auth',
    # ...
]

# admin.py
from django.contrib import admin

class CustomAdminSite(admin.AdminSite):
    # Enable two-factor authentication
    otp_config = 'totp'
    otp_admins = True
```

Tip 6: Implementing Two-Factor Authentication

- Use the `django_otp` package to implement two-factor authentication.
- Consider enabling two-factor authentication for added security, especially for admin users.

Two-factor authentication (2FA) is a security measure that requires users to provide two forms of identification to access the admin interface. To implement 2FA in Django, use a third-party package such as `django-two-factor-auth` or `django-otp`. These packages provide 2FA functionality, including one-time password (OTP) generation, TOTP (time-based OTP), and HOTP (event-based OTP).

Examples and Tips

1. Utilize third-party packages for customization: Third-party packages such as `django-admin-bootstrap` and `django-admin-reorder` provide a convenient and easy way to customize the admin interface's layout, styling, and branding.
2. Override default methods for customization: Overriding default methods in `ModelAdmin` classes allows developers to customize the display and behavior of the admin interface.
3. Implement permission management views: Custom

permission management views can be created to allow users to assign permissions to other users.
4. Use two-factor authentication for increased security: Implementing two-factor authentication provides an additional layer of security for the admin interface.

In this chapter, we've explored advanced customization options for the Django admin interface, including styling and theming, customizing list and detail views, adding custom actions, and implementing security measures. These techniques empower developers to tailor the admin interface to the specific needs of their applications while ensuring robust security practices are in place.

Book Recommendations

App Ideas for the Future; The Next Big Thing: Ultimate Thousands of App Ideas Handbook

FitTech Revolution: The Complete Guide to Developing a Health and Fitness App: From Concept to Success

Chapter 5: Building RESTful APIs with Django Rest Framework

5.1 Introduction to Django Rest Framework

5.1.1 Overview of RESTful APIs

Representational State Transfer (REST) is an architectural style for designing networked applications. In the context of web development, RESTful APIs provide a standardized way for systems to communicate over HTTP. Understanding REST principles is fundamental for effective API design.

RESTful APIs (Representational State Transfer) are web services that utilize HTTP methods (GET, POST, PUT, DELETE) to perform CRUD (Create, Read, Update, Delete) operations on resources. RESTful APIs follow a set of architectural principles, including client-server separation, statelessness, cacheability, and layering.

Key Concepts:

- Resources and URIs: How resources are identified and accessed through Uniform Resource Identifiers.
- HTTP Methods: The use of standard HTTP methods (GET, POST, PUT, DELETE) to perform operations on resources.
- Statelessness: The principle that each request from a client contains all the information needed to

understand and process the request.

Best Practices:

- Designing resource URIs that are meaningful and follow a consistent pattern.
- Using appropriate HTTP methods for different types of operations.

5.1.2 Installing and Configuring DRF

Django Rest Framework (DRF) is a powerful toolkit for building Web APIs in Django. To get started, install DRF using pip:

```
##(CMD/Terminal)
pip install djangorestframework
```

Configure DRF in your Django project by adding it to the INSTALLED_APPS in your settings.py:

```python
python
INSTALLED_APPS = [
    # ...
    'rest_framework',
]
```

Ensure your Django models are ready and then create serializers and views to expose the data through the API.

Example Code:

```python
# serializers.py
from rest_framework import serializers
from .models import YourModel


class YourModelSerializer(serializers.ModelSerializer):
    class Meta:
        model = YourModel
        fields = '__all__'
```

```python
# views.py
from rest_framework import viewsets
from .models import YourModel
from .serializers import YourModelSerializer


class YourModelViewSet(viewsets.ModelViewSet):
    queryset = YourModel.objects.all()
    serializer_class = YourModelSerializer
```

Django Rest Framework (DRF) is a powerful and flexible toolkit for building RESTful APIs in Django. To install DRF, use `pip`:

##(CMD/Tcrminal)

```
pip install djangorestframework
```

To configure DRF, add it to the `INSTALLED_APPS` and `MIDDLEWARE` settings in Django:

python
```python
INSTALLED_APPS = [
    # ...
    'rest_framework',
]

MIDDLEWARE = [
    # ...

'rest_framework.middleware.CommonMiddleware',
]
```

5.2 Serializers and ViewSets

5.2.1 Creating Serializers

Serializers in DRF allow complex data types, such as Django QuerySets and model instances, to be converted to Python data types that can be easily rendered into JSON. Serializers also provide deserialization, allowing parsed data to be converted back into complex types.

Best Practices:

- Define serializers for each model to control how data is presented through the API.
- Leverage validation in serializers to ensure data integrity.

Example Code:

```python
# serializers.py
class YourModelSerializer(serializers.ModelSerializer):
    class Meta:
        model = YourModel
        fields = '__all__'
```

Serializers in DRF convert complex data structures, such as Django models, into JSON or XML format. To create a serializer, use the `serializers.ModelSerializer` class:

```python
from rest_framework import serializers
from .models import MyModel


class MyModelSerializer(serializers.ModelSerializer):
    class Meta:
        model = MyModel
```

```python
    fields = ['field1', 'field2']
```

5.2.2 Using ViewSets for Resource Handling

ViewSets in DRF are classes that provide CRUD operations for models or custom resources. They handle the logic for displaying, creating, updating, and deleting resources.

Best Practices:

- Use `ModelViewSet` to automatically generate views for your models.
- Customize ViewSets for more complex resource handling requirements.

Example Code:

```python
# views.py
from rest_framework import viewsets
from .models import YourModel
from .serializers import YourModelSerializer


class YourModelViewSet(viewsets.ModelViewSet):
    queryset = YourModel.objects.all()
    serializer_class = YourModelSerializer
```

ViewSets in DRF provide a convenient way to handle resources in a RESTful API. To create a ViewSet, use the `viewsets.ModelViewSet` class:

python
```python
from rest_framework import viewsets
from .models import MyModel
from .serializers import MyModelSerializer


class MyModelViewSet(viewsets.ModelViewSet):
    queryset = MyModel.objects.all()
    serializer class = MyModelSerializer
```

5.3 Authentication and Permissions

5.3.1 Implementing Token Authentication

Token authentication is a common method to secure API endpoints. DRF provides a built-in `TokenAuthentication` class that can be added to your project.

Best Practices:

- Use token authentication for secure communication between clients and your API.
- Rotate tokens regularly for enhanced security.

Example Code:

```python
# settings.py
INSTALLED_APPS = [
    # ...
    'rest_framework.authtoken',
]

REST_FRAMEWORK = {
    'DEFAULT_AUTHENTICATION_CLASSES': [

'rest_framework.authentication.TokenAuthentication',
    ],
}
```

Token authentication in DRF provides a simple authentication mechanism using a token-based authentication system. To implement token authentication, add the following to the Django settings:

```python
REST_FRAMEWORK = {
    'DEFAULT_AUTHENTICATION_CLASSES': (

'rest_framework.authentication.TokenAuthentication',
    ),
}
```

To obtain a token for a user, use the

`obtain_auth_token` view provided by DRF:

python

```python
from rest_framework.views import APIView
from rest_framework.authtoken.views
import ObtainAuthToken

class CustomAuthToken(ObtainAuthToken):
    serializer_class =
CustomAuthTokenSerializer

class
CustomAuthTokenSerializer(serializers.Se
rializer):
    username = serializers.CharField()
    password = serializers.CharField()

    def validate(self, attrs):
        user = authenticate(**attrs)
        if user is None:
            raise
serializers.ValidationError('Invalid
credentials')
        attrs['user'] = user
        return attrs
```

5.3.2 Customizing Permissions

Permissions in DRF control access to resources. Customize permissions to suit your application's specific needs.

Best Practices:

- Use the principle of least privilege; only grant the permissions necessary for each user or role.
- Implement custom permissions for fine-grained control.

Example Code:

```python
# permissions.py
from rest_framework import permissions

class IsOwnerOrReadOnly(permissions.BasePermission):
    def has_object_permission(self, request, view, obj):
        return obj.owner == request.user or request.method in permissions.SAFE_METHODS
```

In your views or ViewSets:

```python
# views.py
from rest_framework import viewsets, permissions
from .models import YourModel
from .serializers import YourModelSerializer
from .permissions import
```

```
IsOwnerOrReadOnly

class
YourModelViewSet(viewsets.ModelViewSet):
    queryset = YourModel.objects.all()
    serializer_class =
YourModelSerializer
    permission_classes =
[permissions.IsAuthenticatedOrReadOnly,
IsOwnerOrReadOnly]
```

Tips:

1. **Version Your API:** Include versioning in your API to ensure backward compatibility as your API evolves.
2. **Throttle Your API:** Implement throttling to prevent abuse and ensure fair usage.
3. **Document Your API:** Use tools like Swagger or DRF's built-in documentation to provide clear and comprehensive API documentation.
4. **Use Serializers Wisely:** Serialize only the necessary fields, and consider nested serializers for complex relationships.
5. **Test Your API Endpoints:** Regularly test your API endpoints, including different authentication scenarios and edge cases.

Permissions in DRF control access to resources in a RESTful API. To create a custom permission, subclass the `permissions.BasePermission` class:

python
```python
from rest_framework import permissions

class IsAdminUserOrReadOnly(permissions.BasePermission):
    def has_object_permission(self, request, view, obj):
        if request.method in permissions.SAFE_METHODS:
            return True
        return request.user.is_staff
```

Examples and Tips

1. Use ViewSets for resource handling: ViewSets provide a convenient and flexible way to handle resources in a RESTful API.
2. Customize permissions for fine-grained control: Custom permissions allow developers to control access to resources in a RESTful API.
3. Utilize serializers for data conversion: Serializers convert complex data structures into JSON or XML format, providing a convenient way to handle data in a RESTful API.
4. Implement token authentication for secure access: Token authentication provides a simple and secure way to authenticate users in a RESTful API.

By mastering the concepts of building RESTful APIs with Django Rest Framework, you pave the way for creating robust and scalable web applications with Django. Understanding authentication, permissions, serializers, and ViewSets is crucial for developing APIs that meet modern standards and security requirements. Apply these techniques to elevate your Django development skills and deliver powerful APIs for your projects.

Chapter 6: Asynchronous Django with Channels

Django Channels extends Django to handle asynchronous protocols and adds support for WebSockets, allowing developers to build real-time applications efficiently. In this chapter, we'll explore the fundamentals of asynchronous programming, the installation and configuration of Django Channels, building real-time applications using WebSockets, and considerations for deploying asynchronous Django applications.

6.1 Introduction to Django Channels

6.1.1 Understanding Asynchronous Programming

Asynchronous programming is a programming paradigm that enables non-blocking execution of tasks, allowing multiple tasks to be performed concurrently without waiting for each other to complete. In Django Channels, this is crucial for handling long-lived connections such as WebSockets efficiently.

Example Code 1: Asynchronous Function in Django

```python
python
# views.py
from django.http import HttpResponse
```

```python
import asyncio

async def
asynchronous_function(request):
    # Simulate asynchronous task
    await asyncio.sleep(2)
    return HttpResponse("Task
Completed")
```

Tip 1: Understanding Asynchronous Programming

- Asynchronous programming is beneficial for handling tasks that involve waiting, such as I/O operations, without blocking the entire process.
- Use the `async` and `await` keywords to define and await asynchronous functions.

6.1.2 Installing and Configuring Channels

Installing Django Channels and configuring it to work with your Django project involves a few additional steps compared to a traditional Django setup.

Example Code 2: Installing Django Channels

Django Channels is a toolkit for building asynchronous applications with Django. To install Django Channels, use `pip`:

##(CMD/Terminal)

```
pip install channels
```

To configure Django Channels, add the following to the
Django settings:

python
```
INSTALLED_APPS = [
    # ...
    'channels',
]

ASGI_APPLICATION =
'project.routing.application'
```

Tip 2: Installing and Configuring Channels

- After installing Channels, add `'channels'` to the
  `INSTALLED_APPS` in your Django project settings.
- Configure the project's `asgi.py` file to include
  Channels.

6.2 Building Real-Time Applications

6.2.1 WebSockets and Channels Consumers

WebSockets provide a full-duplex communication channel
over a single, long-lived connection. Django Channels
introduces the concept of consumers, which are similar to
views but handle WebSocket connections and asynchronous

events.

Example Code 3: Implementing a Channels Consumer

```python
# consumers.py
import json
from channels.generic.websocket import AsyncWebsocketConsumer

class RealTimeConsumer(AsyncWebsocketConsumer):
    async def connect(self):
        await self.accept()

    async def disconnect(self, close_code):
        pass

    async def receive(self, text_data):
        data = json.loads(text_data)
        message = data['message']

        await self.send(text_data=json.dumps({'message': message}))
```

WebSockets provide a persistent connection between a client and a server, enabling real-time communication between the two. Channels consumers handle WebSocket connections and provide a convenient way to handle real-time communication in Django.

To create a Channels consumer, use the `consumers.AsyncConsumer` class:

python
```python
import json
from channels.generic.websocket import AsyncWebsocketConsumer

class MyConsumer(AsyncWebsocketConsumer):
    async def connect(self):
        await self.accept()

    async def disconnect(self, close_code):
        pass

    async def receive(self, text_data):
        text_data_json = json.loads(text_data)
        message = text_data_json['message']
        await self.send(text_data=json.dumps({'message': message}))
```

Tip 3: WebSockets and Channels Consumers

- Consumers handle different WebSocket events such as `connect`, `disconnect`, and `receive`.
- Use `self.send()` to send messages to the WebSocket.

6.2.2 Handling Asynchronous Tasks

In asynchronous Django applications, you might need to handle asynchronous tasks efficiently. Django Channels provides tools for this, allowing you to run background tasks alongside WebSocket consumers.

Example Code 4: Handling Asynchronous Tasks with Channels

```python
# consumers.py
from channels.db import database_sync_to_async

class RealTimeConsumer(AsyncWebsocketConsumer):
    async def receive(self, text_data):
        data = json.loads(text_data)
        message = data['message']

        # Asynchronous database operation
        await self.save_message(message)
```

```python
        await self.send(text_data=json.dumps({'message': message}))

    @database_sync_to_async
    def save_message(self, message):
        # Asynchronous database save
        Message.objects.create(content=message)
```

Asynchronous tasks can be handled using the `asgiref` and `celery` libraries. `asgiref` provides support for asynchronous functions in Django, while `celery` provides a distributed task queue for handling asynchronous tasks.

To install `asgiref` and `celery`, use `pip`:

##(CMD/Terminal)
```
pip install asgiref celery
```
To configure `celery`, add the following to the Django settings:

python
```
import os
from celery import Celery

os.environ.setdefault('DJANGO_SETTINGS_MODULE', 'project.settings')

celery_app = Celery('project')
celery_app.config_from_object('django.co
```

```
nf:settings', namespace='CELERY')
celery app.autodiscover_tasks()
```

To create a Celery task, use the `@shared_task` decorator:

python

```python
from celery import shared_task

@shared_task
def my_task():
    # Perform asynchronous task
```

Tip 4: Handling Asynchronous Tasks

- Use `database_sync_to_async` to execute synchronous database operations asynchronously.
- Be cautious with long-running synchronous operations within asynchronous consumers to avoid blocking.

6.3 Deploying Asynchronous Django Applications

6.3.1 Considerations for Deployment

Deploying asynchronous Django applications with Channels introduces specific considerations. Web servers like Daphne are commonly used in production for handling asynchronous connections efficiently.

Example Code 5: Deploying with Daphne

```
##(CMD/Terminal)
pip install daphne
```

Tip 5: Deployment Considerations

- Use an ASGI server like Daphne for deploying Django Channels applications.
- Update your production server configuration to handle ASGI applications.

When deploying asynchronous Django applications, it's important to consider the following factors:

1. Scalability: Asynchronous Django applications can handle a higher volume of requests compared to synchronous applications. Ensure that the deployment environment can handle the increased volume of requests.
2. Load Balancing: Load balancing is essential for distributing incoming requests across multiple servers. This can be achieved using load balancers, such as HAProxy, NGINX, or Amazon ELB.
3. Persistent Connections: WebSocket connections require persistent connections between clients and servers. Ensure that the deployment environment supports persistent connections.

6.3.2 Load Balancing and Scalability

For applications with high traffic or resource-intensive WebSocket connections, load balancing becomes essential. Distributing the load among multiple server instances can enhance scalability.

Example Code 6: Load Balancing with Channels and Redis

```
##(CMD/Terminal)
pip install channels_redis
```

Tip 6: Load Balancing and Scalability

- Use a channel layer backend like Redis to facilitate communication between multiple server instances.
- Update your Django project settings to configure Channels to use Redis as a channel layer.

Load balancing is essential for distributing incoming requests across multiple servers. This can be achieved using load balancers, such as HAProxy, NGINX, or Amazon ELB.

When using load balancers, it's important to consider the following factors:

1. Session Stickiness: Session stickiness ensures that incoming requests from a client are directed to the

same server. This is essential for handling WebSocket connections.
2. Health Checks: Health checks ensure that the load balancer can detect and redirect traffic away from unhealthy servers.
3. SSL Offloading: SSL offloading enables the load balancer to handle SSL encryption and decryption, reducing the load on application servers.

Examples and Tips

1. Utilize WebSockets for real-time communication: WebSockets provide a convenient way to handle real-time communication between clients and servers.
2. Use asynchronous tasks for background processing: Asynchronous tasks provide a convenient way to handle background processing, improving the performance and responsiveness of web applications.
3. Consider deployment factors: When deploying asynchronous Django applications, consider factors such as scalability, load balancing, and persistent connections.

In conclusion, mastering Django Channels is essential for advanced Django development. Adopting these principles can lead to more scalable, responsive, and real-time web applications, improving the user experience for end-users. When working with Django Channels, it's important to consider factors such as WebSockets, asynchronous tasks, and deployment. By utilizing Channels consumers, asynchronous tasks, and load balancing, developers can build asynchronous Django applications that meet the needs of their projects and applications.

In this chapter, we've explored the fundamentals of asynchronous programming, the installation and configuration of Django Channels, building real-time applications using WebSockets and Channels consumers, handling asynchronous tasks, and considerations for deploying asynchronous Django applications. Armed with this knowledge, you can leverage Django Channels to build scalable and real-time features in your Django applications.

Chapter 7: Advanced Testing Techniques

Testing is a crucial aspect of software development to ensure the reliability and correctness of your Django applications. In this chapter, we'll delve into advanced testing techniques, including comprehensive test writing, Test-Driven Development (TDD) principles, and automating tests with Continuous Integration (CI).

7.1 Writing Comprehensive Tests

7.1.1 Test Fixtures and Data Setup

Creating comprehensive tests involves setting up fixtures and data to simulate real-world scenarios. Fixtures are a set of pre-loaded data that the tests use as a baseline.

Example Code 1: Test Fixtures and Data Setup

```python
# tests.py
from django.test import TestCase
from django.contrib.auth.models import User

class MyModelTests(TestCase):
    @classmethod
    def setUpTestData(cls):
        # Set up test data
```

```python
        User.objects.create(username='testuser',
email='test@example.com',
password='testpassword')

    def test_example(self):
        # Your test logic using the set-
up data
        user =
User.objects.get(username='testuser')
        self.assertEqual(user.email,
'test@example.com')
```

Tip 1: Test Fixtures and Data Setup

- Utilize `setUpTestData` for setting up data that
  remains consistent across all test methods in the test
  case.
- Keep test data separate from production data to
  maintain test independence.

Test fixtures and data setup are essential components of
comprehensive testing in Django. Test fixtures provide a set
of initial data that can be used to test the behavior of views,
forms, and models. Data setup involves creating and
manipulating data in the database to test various scenarios.

Test fixtures can be created using the `fixtures` directory
in the Django app. To create a test fixture, create a JSON or

YAML file containing the data to be loaded:

yaml

```
[
    {
        "model": "app.model",
        "pk": 1,
        "fields": {
            "field1": "value1",
            "field2": "value2"
        }
    }
]
```

Data setup can be performed using Django's test database and the `setUpTestData` method:

python

```
from django.test import TestCase
from django.contrib.auth.models import User

class MyTestCase(TestCase):
    setUpTestData = classmethod(setUpTestData)

    @classmethod
    def setUpTestData(cls):
        cls.user = User.objects.create_user(username='testuser', password='testpassword')
```

7.1.2 Testing Views, Forms, and Models

Django provides tools to test views, forms, and models comprehensively. Each type of test ensures that specific components of your application are functioning as expected.

Example Code 2: Testing Views, Forms, and Models

```python
# tests.py
from django.test import TestCase
from django.urls import reverse
from django.contrib.auth.models import User
from myapp.models import MyModel
from myapp.forms import MyForm

class MyViewTests(TestCase):
    def test_view_returns_correct_status_code(self):
        response = self.client.get(reverse('myapp:my_view'))

        self.assertEqual(response.status_code, 200)

class MyFormTests(TestCase):
    def test_form_is_valid(self):
        form_data = {'field_name':
```

```python
'value'}
        form = MyForm(data=form_data)
        self.assertTrue(form.is_valid())

class MyModelTests(TestCase):
    def test_model_method(self):
        user =
User.objects.create(username='testuser',
email='test@example.com',
password='testpassword')
        my_model =
MyModel.objects.create(user=user,
some_field='value')

self.assertEqual(my_model.custom_method(
), 'expected result')
```

Tip 2: Testing Views, Forms, and Models

- Use the Django testing client to simulate HTTP requests and test views.
- Ensure that form and model tests cover both valid and invalid scenarios.

Testing views, forms, and models is essential for ensuring the correct behavior of Django applications. Views can be tested using Django's test client, while forms and models can be tested using Django's testing framework.

To test a view, use the test client to make a request to the view and assert the expected response:

python
```python
from django.test import TestCase
from django.test.client import Client

class MyTestCase(TestCase):
    def test_view(self):
        client = Client()
        response = client.get('/my-view/')

self.assertEqual(response.status_code, 200)
        self.assertContains(response, 'Expected text')
```

To test a form, use the `form_class` attribute to create an instance of the form and assert the expected behavior:

python
```python
from django.test import TestCase
from .forms import MyForm

class MyTestCase(TestCase):
    def test_form(self):
        form = MyForm(data={'field1': 'value1', 'field2': 'value2'})
        self.assertTrue(form.is_valid())
```

To test a model, use the `setUpTestData` method to create data in the test database and assert the expected behavior:

python

```python
from django.test import TestCase
from .models import MyModel

class MyTestCase(TestCase):
    setUpTestData =
classmethod(setUpTestData)

    @classmethod
    def setUpTestData(cls):

MyModel.objects.create(field1='value1',
field2='value2')

    def test_model(self):
        my_model =
MyModel.objects.get(pk=1)

self.assertEqual(my_model.field1,
'value1')

self.assertEqual(my_model.field2,
'value2')
```

7.2 Test-Driven Development (TDD)

7.2.1 TDD Principles and Workflow

Test-Driven Development (TDD) is a development

approach where tests are written before the actual code. This methodology encourages iterative development and ensures that each piece of code is thoroughly tested.

Test-Driven Development (TDD) is a software development approach that involves writing tests before writing the actual code. TDD follows a simple workflow:

1. Write a test for a specific functionality.
2. Run the test to ensure that it fails.
3. Write the actual code to pass the test.
4. Run the test to ensure that it passes.
5. Refactor the code if necessary.

TDD promotes a disciplined approach to software development, ensuring that code is testable, maintainable, and well-designed.

Example Code 3: Test-Driven Development Workflow

```python
# tests.py
from django.test import TestCase
from myapp.models import MyModel

class MyModelTests(TestCase):
    def test_model_method(self):
        my_model =
MyModel.objects.create(some_field='value
')
```

```python
    self.assertEqual(my_model.custom_method(
), 'expected result')
```

Tip 3: TDD Principles and Workflow

- Follow the Red-Green-Refactor cycle: write a failing test (Red), make the test pass (Green), and then refactor the code.
- TDD helps in designing modular and testable code from the beginning.

7.2.2 Real-World TDD Example

Let's consider a real-world example of implementing a new feature using TDD. Suppose we want to add a new API endpoint for creating a resource.

Example Code 4: Real-World TDD Example

```python
python
# tests.py
from django.test import TestCase
from django.urls import reverse
from rest_framework.test import APIClient
from myapp.models import MyModel

class MyApiTests(TestCase):
    def
test_create_resource_endpoint(self):
```

```python
        client = APIClient()
        data = {'field_name': 'value'}
        response =
client.post(reverse('myapp:create_resour
ce'), data, format='json')

self.assertEqual(response.status_code,
201)

self.assertEqual(MyModel.objects.count()
, 1)
```

Tip 4: Real-World TDD Example

- Start with a test for the new feature.
- Write the minimal code required to make the test pass.
- Gradually enhance the functionality while ensuring all tests pass.

Consider the following example of TDD for a Django application:

1. Write a test for a view that displays a list of objects:

python
```python
from django.test import TestCase
from django.test.client import Client


class MyViewTestCase(TestCase):
    def test_view(self):
        client = Client()
```

```python
        response = client.get('/my-view/')

self.assertEqual(response.status_code, 200)
        self.assertContains(response, 'Expected text')
```

2.   Run the test to ensure that it fails:


```
python manage.py test
```

3.   Write the actual code to pass the test:

python
```python
from django.shortcuts import render
from .models import MyModel

def my_view(request):
    objects = MyModel.objects.all()
    return render(request, 'my-view.html', {'objects': objects})
```

4.   Run the test to ensure that it passes:


```
python manage.py test
```

5.   Refactor the code if necessary.

7.3 Automated Testing with Continuous Integration

7.3.1 Setting Up CI/CD Pipelines

Continuous Integration (CI) ensures that code changes are automatically tested and validated whenever pushed to the version control repository. This practice catches issues early in the development process.

Example Code 5: Setting Up CI/CD Pipelines with GitHub Actions

```yaml
# .github/workflows/main.yml
name: CI

on: [push, pull_request]

jobs:
  test:
    runs-on: ubuntu-latest

    steps:
    - name: Checkout repository
      uses: actions/checkout@v2

    - name: Set up Python
      uses: actions/setup-python@v2
      with:
        python-version: 3.8

    - name: Install dependencies
```

```yaml
    run: |
      pip install -r requirements.txt

  - name: Run tests
    run: |
      python manage.py test
```

Tip 5: Setting Up CI/CD Pipelines

- Leverage CI tools like GitHub Actions, GitLab CI, or Travis CI for automated testing.
- Include steps for installing dependencies and running tests in your CI configuration.

Continuous Integration (CI) and Continuous Deployment (CD) pipelines enable automated testing and deployment of Django applications. CI/CD pipelines can be set up using popular services, such as GitHub Actions, Travis CI, or CircleCI.

To set up a CI/CD pipeline, create a configuration file that defines the pipeline:

yaml

```yaml
name: Django CI/CD

on:
  push:
    branches:
      - main
  pull_request:
```

```yaml
    branches:
      - main

jobs:
  test:
    runs-on: ubuntu-latest
    steps:
      - uses: actions/checkout@v2
      - name: Set up Python
        uses: actions/setup-python@v2
        with:
          python-version: 3.9
      - name: Install dependencies
        run: |
          python -m pip install --upgrade pip
          pip install -r requirements.txt
      - name: Run tests
        run: python manage.py test
```

7.3.2 Integrating with Popular CI Services

Integrating Django projects with popular CI services
ensures that tests are automatically run on each code
change, providing continuous feedback to the development
team.

Example Code 6: Integrating with Travis CI

```yaml
# .travis.yml
```

```yaml
language: python
python:
  - "3.8"

install:
  - pip install -r requirements.txt

script:
  - python manage.py test
```

Tip 6: Integrating with Popular CI Services

- Customize CI configurations based on your project's requirements.
- Integrate CI with version control services such as GitHub, GitLab, or Bitbucket.

Popular CI services, such as GitHub Actions, Travis CI, or CircleCI, provide convenient ways to set up CI/CD pipelines for Django applications.

GitHub Actions provides a simple and convenient way to set up CI/CD pipelines for Django applications hosted on GitHub. To set up a GitHub Actions workflow, create a `.github/workflows/` directory and create a YAML file that defines the workflow:

yaml
```yaml
name: Django CI/CD
```

```yaml
on:
  push:
    branches:
      - main
  pull_request:
    branches:
      - main

jobs:
  test:
    runs-on: ubuntu-latest
    steps:
      - uses: actions/checkout@v2
      - name: Set up Python
        uses: actions/setup-python@v2
        with:
          python-version: 3.9
      - name: Install dependencies
        run: |
          python -m pip install --upgrade pip
          pip install -r requirements.txt
      - name: Run tests
        run: python manage.py test
```

Examples and Tips

1. Utilize test fixtures and data setup: Test fixtures and
   data setup provide a convenient way to set up data for
   testing views, forms, and models.

2. Follow TDD principles and workflow: TDD promotes a disciplined approach to software development, ensuring that code is testable, maintainable, and well-designed.
3. Set up CI/CD pipelines: CI/CD pipelines provide automated testing and deployment of Django applications, improving the reliability and maintainability of the application.

In conclusion, mastering advanced testing techniques is essential for advanced Django development. Adopting these principles can lead to more testable, maintainable, and reliable web applications. When working with Django, it's important to consider test fixtures, data setup, TDD, and automated testing with CI/CD pipelines. By utilizing comprehensive tests, TDD, and CI/CD pipelines, developers can build high-quality Django applications that meet the needs of their projects and applications.

In this chapter, we've explored advanced testing techniques, including writing comprehensive tests, Test-Driven Development (TDD) principles, and automating tests with Continuous Integration (CI). Implementing these techniques ensures the robustness and reliability of your Django applications, fostering a culture of continuous improvement in software development practices.

Chapter 8: Performance Optimization Strategies

Efficient performance is crucial for the success of any web application. In this chapter, we'll delve into advanced strategies for optimizing the performance of Django applications, covering profiling, caching techniques, and database optimization.

8.1 Profiling Django Applications

8.1.1 Identifying Bottlenecks

Profiling your Django application helps identify performance bottlenecks, allowing you to focus on optimizing specific areas. Python provides built-in profiling tools, such as `cProfile`, which can be integrated into Django projects.

Performance optimization is an essential aspect of web development, and Django provides various tools and techniques to optimize the performance of web applications. The first step in performance optimization is identifying bottlenecks in the application, which can be done using profiling tools.

Example Code 1: Profiling with cProfile

```python
# manage.py
import cProfile
from django.core.management import execute_from_command_line

if __name__ == "__main__":

cProfile.run('execute_from_command_line(
["manage.py", "runserver"])',
sort='cumulative')
```

Tip 1: Identifying Bottlenecks

- Focus on the most time-consuming functions identified by profiling.
- Use profiling in development to avoid the overhead of profiling in production.

Django provides a built-in profiling tool, the `django.core.profilers` module, which can be used to profile views, templates, and other parts of the application. To use the profiler, import the `ProfileMiddleware` and add it to the `MIDDLEWARE` setting:

python

```python
MIDDLEWARE = [
    # ...

'django.core.profilers.ProfileMiddleware
',
]
```

Once the profiler is enabled, Django will generate profiling data for each request, which can be accessed through the REQUEST_PROFILER setting:

python

```python
import pprint
from django.http import JsonResponse


def profiler_output(request):
    profiler_data =
request.session.pop('_profiler_data',
[])
    response_data = {'profiler_data':
profiler_data}
    return JsonResponse(response_data)
```

8.1.2 Using Django Debug Toolbar

Django Debug Toolbar is a powerful tool for profiling Django views, displaying detailed information about the time spent on each component of a request-response cycle.

Example Code 2: Installing and Configuring Django Debug Toolbar

```
##(CMD/Terminal)
pip install django-debug-toolbar
```

```python
# settings.py
if DEBUG:
    INSTALLED_APPS += ['debug_toolbar']
    MIDDLEWARE +=
['debug_toolbar.middleware.DebugToolbarM
iddleware']
```

Django Debug Toolbar displays various statistics, including SQL queries, cache hits and misses, and memory usage, providing insights into the performance of the application.

To install Django Debug Toolbar, use `pip`:

```
##(CMD/Terminal)
pip install django-debug-toolbar
```

To configure Django Debug Toolbar, add the following to the Django settings:

```python
INSTALLED_APPS = [
    # ...
    'debug_toolbar',
]
```

```python
MIDDLEWARE = [
    # ...

'debug_toolbar.middleware.DebugToolbarMi
ddleware',
]

INTERNAL_IPS = [
    '127.0.0.1',
]
```

Django Debug Toolbar provides a convenient way to profile
the performance of web applications, providing insights
into bottlenecks and areas for optimization.

Tip 2: Using Django Debug Toolbar

- Utilize the toolbar to analyze SQL queries, template
  rendering times, and overall request processing.
- Enable the toolbar in development settings only to
  avoid security risks in production.

8.2 Caching Techniques

8.2.1 Django Caching Framework

Django's caching framework allows you to store and
retrieve the results of expensive function calls, database
queries, or calculated values.

Django provides a caching framework that enables caching

of various parts of the application, including views, templates, and database queries. Caching can significantly improve the performance of web applications, reducing the number of requests and the amount of processing required.

Example Code 3: Using Django Caching Framework

```python
# views.py
from django.views.decorators.cache import cache_page

@cache_page(60 * 15)  # Cache for 15 minutes
def my_view(request):
    # Your view logic
    return HttpResponse("Cached Response")
```

Tip 3: Django Caching Framework

- Apply caching to views that involve heavy computations or database queries.
- Configure cache timeouts based on the frequency of data updates.

Django provides various caching backends, including file-based, database, and in-memory caching. To use Django's caching framework, add the following to the Django settings:

python

```python
CACHES = {
    'default': {
        'BACKEND':
'django.core.cache.backends.memcached.MemcachedCache',
        'LOCATION': '127.0.0.1:11211',
    }
}
```

To cache a view, use the `@cache_page` decorator:

python

```python
from django.views.decorators.cache import cache_page

@cache_page(60 * 15)
def my_view(request):
    # ...
```

8.2.2 Implementing Cache Invalidation

Cache invalidation is crucial to ensure that stale data is not served to users. Django provides tools for cache versioning and dynamic cache key generation.

Cache invalidation is the process of invalidating or deleting cached data when the underlying data changes. Cache invalidation is essential to ensure that the application displays up-to-date data.

Django provides various techniques for cache invalidation, including using the `django.core.cache.cache.delete` method to delete cached data and using the `django.core.cache.cache.set` method to set a cache timeout.

Example Code 4: Cache Invalidation with Cache Versioning

```python
# settings.py
CACHES = {
    'default': {
        'BACKEND':
'django.core.cache.backends.memcached.MemcachedCache',
        'LOCATION': '127.0.0.1:11211',
        'VERSION': 1,  # Increment version when changes occur
    }
}
```

Tip 4: Implementing Cache Invalidation

- Use cache versioning to invalidate all cache keys

when a significant change occurs.
- Combine cache with cache decorators, like `cache_page` and `cache_control`, for more granular control.

To implement cache invalidation, use the `post_save` signal to trigger cache deletion when the underlying data changes:

python
```python
from django.db.models.signals import post_save
from django.dispatch import receiver
from django.core.cache import cache
from .models import MyModel


@receiver(post_save, sender=MyModel)
def my_model_post_save(sender, instance, **kwargs):
    cache.delete('my_model_cache')
```

8.3 Database Optimization

8.3.1 Query Optimization Tips

Optimizing database queries is crucial for enhancing overall application performance. Techniques like using `select_related` and `prefetch_related` can minimize the number of database queries.

Database optimization is an essential aspect of performance optimization in Django. Django provides various tools and techniques to optimize database queries, including query optimization tips and querysets.

When optimizing database queries, it's important to consider the following tips:

1. Avoid using the `select_related` method for non-related fields.
2. Use the `prefetch_related` method to fetch related objects in a separate query.
3. Use the `only` method to fetch only the required fields.
4. Use the `defer` method to defer loading of non-required fields.
5. Use the `values` method to fetch only the required fields as dictionaries.

Example Code 5: Query Optimization with `select_related` and `prefetch_related`

```python
# views.py
from django.shortcuts import render
from myapp.models import Author, Book

def my_view(request):
    authors = Author.objects.select_related('profile').all()
```

```python
    books =
Book.objects.prefetch_related('genres').
all()
    return render(request,
'template.html', {'authors': authors,
'books': books})
```

Tip 5: Query Optimization Tips

- Use `select_related` for ForeignKey relationships and `prefetch_related` for ManyToMany relationships to minimize queries.
- Limit the use of `defer()` and `only()` to fetch only the necessary fields.

8.3.2 Indexing and Querysets

Properly indexing your database tables can significantly improve query performance. Django provides tools to inspect and optimize database queries.

Example Code 6: Indexing Database Fields

```python
python
# models.py
from django.db import models

class MyModel(models.Model):
    name =
models.CharField(max length=255,
```

```python
db_index=True)
    description = models.TextField()
```

Tip 6: Indexing and Querysets

- Use `db_index=True` to add an index to fields that are frequently used in queries.
- Use Django Debug Toolbar to analyze and optimize queries during development.

Indexing is an essential aspect of database optimization, improving the performance of database queries. Django provides a convenient way to create indexes using the `db_index` attribute:

python
```python
class MyModel(models.Model):
    field1 = models.CharField(max_length=100, db_index=True)
```

When optimizing querysets, it's important to consider the following tips:

1. Use the `filter` method instead of the `exclude` method.
2. Use the `get` method instead of the `filter` method for single objects.
3. Use the `exists` method to check if an object exists.

4. Use the `count` method to count the number of objects.
5. Use the `distinct` method to eliminate duplicate objects.

Examples and Tips

1. Utilize profiling tools: Profiling tools, such as Django's built-in profiler and Django Debug Toolbar, provide insights into the performance of web applications, enabling developers to optimize the performance of the application.
2. Use caching techniques: Caching techniques, such as Django's caching framework, provide a convenient way to cache various parts of the application, reducing the number of requests and the amount of processing required.
3. Optimize database queries: Database optimization is essential for improving the performance of web applications. Django provides various tools and techniques to optimize database queries, including query optimization tips and querysets.

In conclusion, mastering performance optimization strategies is essential for advanced Django development. Adopting these principles can lead to faster, more efficient web applications. When working with Django, it's important to consider profiling, caching, and database optimization techniques. By utilizing profiling tools, caching techniques, and optimized querysets, developers can build high-performance Django applications that meet the needs of their projects and applications.

In this chapter, we've explored advanced strategies for optimizing Django application performance. From profiling and caching techniques to database optimization, these strategies empower developers to build high-performance and scalable Django applications. By implementing these techniques judiciously, you can ensure your application delivers a responsive and efficient user experience.

Book Recommendations

If you are Beginner or Professional Writer, I will recommend any of these books to you.

- **If you want to start writing or you are a Non-Friction Writer**

The Future of Writing and Selling Books: A Guide to ChatGPT-3 AI Technology

How to Get Rich with ChatGPT and Amazon KDP: Unlocking the Power of AI and Self-Publishing to Grow Your Wealth

Chapter 9: Building Scalable Django Applications

Scalability is crucial for ensuring that your Django applications can handle increased load and traffic as they grow. In this chapter, we'll explore strategies for building scalable Django applications, including horizontal scaling, integration with Content Delivery Networks (CDNs), and handling traffic spikes and failovers.

9.1 Scaling Django Horizontally

Scaling Django horizontally involves adding more servers to handle increased traffic and workloads. Scaling horizontally enables web applications to handle a larger volume of traffic and provides high availability and fault tolerance.

9.1.1 Load Balancing Strategies

Horizontal scaling involves distributing incoming requests across multiple servers to improve performance and handle increased traffic. Load balancing ensures that each server receives a manageable workload.

Load balancing strategies include:

1. Round Robin Load Balancing: Distributes incoming traffic evenly across all servers.
2. Least Connections Load Balancing: Distributes incoming traffic to the server with the fewest active connections.
3. IP Hash Load Balancing: Distributes incoming traffic based on the client's IP address.
4. Least Response Time Load Balancing: Distributes incoming traffic to the server with the lowest response time.

To implement load balancing in Django, use a load balancer, such as HAProxy or NGINX, and configure it to distribute incoming traffic across multiple servers.

Example Code 1: Load Balancing with Nginx

```nginx
nginx
# nginx.conf
http {
    upstream django {
        server 127.0.0.1:8000;
        server 127.0.0.1:8001;
        server 127.0.0.1:8002;
    }

    server {
```

```
        listen 80;
        server_name example.com;

        location / {
            proxy_pass http://django;
        }
    }
}
```

Tip 1: Load Balancing Strategies

- Consider using a dedicated load balancer like Nginx or HAProxy to distribute traffic evenly.
- Monitor server performance and adjust load balancing configurations as needed.

9.1.2 Distributed Databases

As your Django application scales, a single database server may become a bottleneck. Distributed databases distribute data across multiple servers, allowing for improved performance and fault tolerance.

Distributed databases enable web applications to handle increased traffic by distributing the database workload across multiple servers. Distributed databases provide high availability and fault tolerance, reducing the risk of downtime and data loss.

To implement distributed databases in Django, use a

distributed database system, such as MySQL Cluster or PostgreSQL Cluster, and configure it to distribute the database workload across multiple servers.

Example Code 2: Using Django with a Distributed Database (Cassandra)

```python
# settings.py
DATABASES = {
    'default': {
        'ENGINE':
'django.db.backends.cassandra',
        'NAME': 'mydatabase',
        'USER': 'myuser',
        'PASSWORD': 'mypassword',
        'HOST': '127.0.0.1',
        'PORT': '9042',
    }
}
```

Tip 2: Distributed Databases

- Evaluate distributed database options such as Cassandra, MongoDB, or CockroachDB based on your application requirements.
- Ensure data consistency and replication across nodes in the distributed database cluster.

9.2 Content Delivery Networks (CDN) Integration

Content Delivery Networks (CDNs) provide a way to improve the delivery of static assets, such as images, videos, and JavaScript files. CDNs distribute static assets across multiple servers, reducing the load on the web application and improving the user experience.

9.2.1 Improving Static Asset Delivery

Integrating a Content Delivery Network (CDN) improves the delivery speed of static assets like images, CSS, and JavaScript files by caching them on edge servers located closer to users.

CDNs improve the delivery of static assets by caching them on servers close to the user's location. CDNs reduce the load on the web application, improving the user experience and reducing the risk of downtime.

To integrate a CDN in Django, configure the web application to serve static assets from the CDN. Configure the CDN to cache static assets and distribute them across multiple servers.

Example Code 3: Integrating Django with a CDN (Amazon CloudFront)

```python
# settings.py
STATIC_URL = 'https://cdn.example.com/static/'
```

Tip 3: CDN Best Practices

- Utilize cache-control headers to control caching behavior and cache invalidation.
- Regularly monitor CDN performance and adjust caching settings as needed.

9.2.2 CDN Best Practices

To maximize the benefits of CDN integration, follow best practices for configuration and optimization.

CDN best practices include:

1. Use a reputable CDN provider.
2. Configure the CDN to cache static assets.
3. Use HTTPS to secure the delivery of static assets.
4. Monitor the CDN's performance and adjust caching settings as necessary.

Tip 4: CDN Best Practices

- Use a separate subdomain or domain for serving static assets via CDN to maximize parallel downloads.
- Enable gzip compression for static assets to reduce file size and improve transfer speed.

9.3 Handling Traffic Spikes and Failovers

Handling traffic spikes and failovers is essential for ensuring the availability and reliability of web applications. Traffic spikes and failovers can occur due to various reasons, including sudden increases in traffic, hardware failures, and network outages.

9.3.1 Strategies for Traffic Management

Traffic spikes can overwhelm your Django application if not handled properly. Implementing traffic management strategies ensures that your application remains responsive during peak load times.

Traffic management strategies include:

1. Use a load balancer to distribute incoming traffic.
2. Use a Content Delivery Network (CDN) to distribute static assets.
3. Use a distributed database system to distribute the database workload.
4. Use caching techniques to reduce the load on the web application.

Tip 5: Traffic Management Strategies

- Implement rate limiting and request throttling to prevent server overload during traffic spikes.

- Use caching layers and CDN caching to offload traffic from the origin server.

9.3.2 Implementing Failover Mechanisms

Failover mechanisms ensure high availability by automatically redirecting traffic to standby servers or backup systems in case of server failures or downtime.

Failover mechanisms provide a way to automatically switch to a standby server in the event of a failure. Failover mechanisms enable web applications to handle failures and continue operating without interruption.

To implement failover mechanisms in Django, use a load balancer with health checks and automatic failover. Configure the load balancer to monitor the health of each server and switch to a standby server in the event of a failure.

Examples and Tips

1. Utilize load balancing strategies: Load balancing strategies provide a convenient way to distribute incoming traffic across multiple servers, improving performance and reliability.
2. Implement distributed databases: Distributed databases enable web applications to handle increased traffic by distributing the database workload across multiple servers.

3. Integrate a CDN: CDNs improve the delivery of static assets, reducing the load on the web application and improving the user experience.
4. Implement failover mechanisms: Failover mechanisms enable web applications to handle failures and continue operating without interruption.

Tip 6: Failover Mechanisms

- Use a multi-region setup with DNS failover to redirect traffic to healthy servers in alternate regions during outages.
- Implement automated monitoring and alerting systems to detect and respond to server failures promptly.

In conclusion, building scalable Django applications involves implementing various strategies and techniques, including load balancing, distributed databases, CDN integration, and failover mechanisms. By utilizing these strategies and techniques, developers can build high-performance and reliable Django applications that meet the needs of their projects and applications. When working with Django, it's important to consider scalability and implement strategies and techniques to handle increased traffic and workloads. By implementing these strategies and techniques, developers can build scalable Django applications that provide high availability and fault tolerance, improving the user experience and reducing the risk of downtime and data loss.

In this chapter, we've explored strategies for building scalable Django applications, including horizontal scaling, CDN integration, and handling traffic spikes and failovers. By implementing these strategies effectively, you can ensure that your Django applications can handle increased load and provide a reliable user experience even as they grow in popularity and complexity.

Chapter 10: Advanced Security Practices

Ensuring robust security is paramount for any Django application. In this chapter, we'll delve into advanced security practices to protect your application from common vulnerabilities, including Cross-Site Scripting (XSS), Cross-Site Request Forgery (CSRF), and implementing security headers.

As web applications become increasingly complex, they introduce new security risks that can leave them vulnerable to attacks. Implementing security best practices is essential for ensuring the safety and integrity of web applications. In this chapter, we will discuss advanced security practices that can help protect Django applications from various types of attacks.

10.1 Cross-Site Scripting (XSS) Prevention

Cross-Site Scripting (XSS) is a type of attack that injects malicious scripts into web pages viewed by unsuspecting users. XSS attacks can result in account takeover, data theft, and other security breaches. To prevent XSS attacks, it's essential to sanitize user input and set appropriate Content Security Policy (CSP) headers.

10.1.1 Sanitizing User Input

Cross-Site Scripting (XSS) is a prevalent attack vector where malicious scripts are injected into web pages. Properly sanitizing user input helps prevent this security risk.

Sanitizing user input is the process of removing or encoding any potentially harmful characters that could be used to inject malicious scripts. Django provides several built-in functions for sanitizing user input, including `escape`, `escapejs`, and `force_text`. These functions can be used to escape special characters, encode HTML entities, and convert non-text data to plain text.

When sanitizing user input, it's important to consider the context in which the input will be used. For example, input that will be used in an HTML attribute requires different sanitization than input that will be used in a script tag.

Example Code 1: Using Django's `mark_safe` to Sanitize HTML

```python
# views.py
from django.utils.safestring import
```

```python
mark_safe

def my_view(request):
    user_input =
request.GET.get('input', '')
    sanitized_input =
mark_safe(user_input)
    return render(request,
'template.html', {'user_input':
sanitized_input})
```

Tip 1: Sanitizing User Input

- Avoid using `mark_safe` for untrusted input to prevent potential XSS vulnerabilities.
- Utilize Django template filters such as `escape` to automatically escape user input in templates.

10.1.2 Using Content Security Policy (CSP)

Content Security Policy (CSP) is an additional layer of defense against XSS attacks. It defines a set of rules to control which resources can be loaded and executed.

Content Security Policy (CSP) is a security feature that allows web applications to specify which resources are allowed to be loaded and executed by the browser. By setting a strict CSP, web applications can prevent XSS attacks by restricting the sources from which scripts can be loaded.

Example Code 2: Implementing Content Security Policy (CSP)

```python
# settings.py
CSP_HEADER = {
    'default-src': "'self'",
    'script-src': ["'self'", "https://cdn.example.com"],
    'style-src': ["'self'", "https://fonts.googleapis.com"],
    'font-src': ["'self'", "https://fonts.gstatic.com"],
}
```

To set a CSP in Django, use the `Content-Security-Policy` header in the response object. The CSP should include a list of allowed sources for scripts, styles, images, and other resources. Here's an example of a CSP that allows scripts only from the application's origin:

```python
response['Content-Security-Policy'] = "script-src 'self'; style-src 'self'; img-src 'self';"
```

Tip 2: Using Content Security Policy (CSP)

- Specify valid sources for scripts, styles, and other

resources in the CSP header.
- Regularly review and update the CSP policy based on your application's requirements.

10.2 Cross-Site Request Forgery (CSRF) Protection

Cross-Site Request Forgery (CSRF) is a type of attack that tricks users into performing actions they didn't intend to perform. CSRF attacks can result in unauthorized actions, such as changing passwords or transferring funds. Django provides built-in CSRF protection that can help prevent CSRF attacks.

10.2.1 Django's Built-in CSRF Protection

Django provides built-in protection against Cross-Site Request Forgery (CSRF) attacks. This protection includes a middleware that generates and validates a unique token for each user session.

Django's built-in CSRF protection works by adding a hidden CSRF token to forms and verifying the token on submission. The CSRF token is a unique value that is generated for each user session and stored in a cookie. When a user submits a form, the CSRF token is included in the request headers. Django verifies the token to ensure that the request is legitimate.

To use Django's built-in CSRF protection, ensure that the `{% csrf_token %}` template tag is included in all forms that perform state-changing actions. Django will automatically include the CSRF token and verify it on submission.

Example Code 3: Enabling CSRF Protection in Django Forms

```python
# forms.py
from django import forms

class MyForm(forms.Form):
    my_field = forms.CharField()


# template.html
<form method="post" action="{% url 'my_view' %}">
  {% csrf_token %}
  {{ form }}
  <button type="submit">Submit</button>
</form>
```

Tip 3: Django's Built-in CSRF Protection

- Ensure that `{% csrf_token %}` is included in all POST forms to protect against CSRF attacks.
- Utilize the `@csrf_exempt` decorator sparingly and only when necessary.

10.2.2 Enhancing CSRF Security

Enhance CSRF security by implementing additional measures such as using the `SameSite` cookie attribute and customizing the CSRF token.

While Django's built-in CSRF protection is effective, it's important to take additional measures to enhance CSRF security. One way to enhance CSRF security is to use a custom CSRF token that is specific to each user session. Using a custom CSRF token can help prevent CSRF attacks by ensuring that the token is unique to each user.

Example Code 4: Enhancing CSRF Security with SameSite Attribute

```python
# settings.py
CSRF_COOKIE_SECURE = True
CSRF_COOKIE_SAMESITE = 'Strict'
```

To use a custom CSRF token, create a custom middleware class that generates and stores a unique token for each user session. Here's an example of a custom CSRF middleware class:

```python
class CustomCSRFMiddleware:
    def __init__(self, get_response):
        self.get_response = get_response
```

```python
    def __call__(self, request):
        if 'CSRF_TOKEN' not in
request.session:

request.session['CSRF_TOKEN'] =
uuid.uuid4().hex
        response =
self.get_response(request)

response.set_cookie(key='CSRF_TOKEN',
value=request.session['CSRF_TOKEN'])
        return response
```

Tip 4: Enhancing CSRF Security

- Set `CSRF_COOKIE_SECURE = True` to ensure
  the CSRF cookie is only sent over HTTPS.
- Adjust `CSRF_COOKIE_SAMESITE` based on your
  application's security requirements.

10.3 Security Headers and Best Practices

Security headers are HTTP response headers that provide
additional security features for web applications.
Implementing security headers can help prevent various
types of attacks, such as XSS and CSRF attacks.

10.3.1 HTTP Security Headers

HTTP security headers provide an extra layer of defense by

controlling browser behavior and mitigating certain types of attacks. Common headers include `Strict-Transport-Security` and `X-Content-Type-Options`.

Here are some common HTTP security headers and their functions:

- `Content-Security-Policy`: Specifies which resources are allowed to be loaded and executed by the browser.
- `X-Content-Type-Options`: Prevents MIME-sniffing attacks by specifying the MIME type of the response.
- `X-Frame-Options`: Prevents clickjacking attacks by specifying whether the page can be embedded in a frame or iframe.
- `Strict-Transport-Security`: Enforces the use of HTTPS by specifying a minimum secure connection period.
- `X-XSS-Protection`: Enables the browser's built-in XSS protection.
- `Referrer-Policy`: Specifies how much referrer information should be included in requests.

Example Code 5: Implementing Strict Transport Security (HSTS)

```python
# settings.py
SECURE_HSTS_SECONDS = 31536000  # 1 year
SECURE_HSTS_INCLUDE_SUBDOMAINS = True
```

Tip 5: HTTP Security Headers

- Enable HSTS to force secure connections and prevent man-in-the-middle attacks.
- Regularly review and update security headers to align with the latest best practices.

To set security headers in Django, use the `Response` object's `set_header` method. Here's an example of setting security headers in Django:

python
```python
response = HttpResponse("Hello, world!")
response['Content-Security-Policy'] =
"default-src 'self'"
response['X-Content-Type-Options'] =
"nosniff"
response['X-Frame-Options'] = "DENY"
response['Strict-Transport-Security'] =
"max-age=31536000; includeSubDomains"
response['X-XSS-Protection'] = "1;
mode=block"
response['Referrer-Policy'] = "strict-
origin-when-cross-origin"
return response
```

10.3.2 Keeping Dependencies Secure

Regularly update and audit your project's dependencies to address security vulnerabilities in third-party libraries.

Tip 6: Keeping Dependencies Secure

- Subscribe to security mailing lists for the libraries you use.
- Use tools like `safety` or `pyup.io` to scan for vulnerabilities in your project dependencies.

Keeping dependencies secure is essential for ensuring the security of web applications. Dependencies can introduce security vulnerabilities if they are not up-to-date or properly configured. Here are some best practices for keeping dependencies secure:

- Keep dependencies up-to-date: Regularly update dependencies to ensure that they are not vulnerable to known security issues.
- Use a package manager: Use a package manager, such as pip or conda, to manage dependencies and ensure that they are properly installed and configured.
- Use a virtual environment: Use a virtual environment, such as virtualenv or conda env, to isolate dependencies and prevent conflicts.
- Use a security scanner: Use a security scanner, such as Snyk or OWASP Dependency-Check, to scan dependencies for known vulnerabilities.
- Limit the use of third-party packages: Limit the use of third-party packages to those that are necessary

and well-maintained.

Examples and Tips

1. Sanitize user input: Sanitize user input to prevent XSS attacks.
2. Use Content Security Policy: Use Content Security Policy to restrict the sources of resources loaded by the browser.
3. Use Django's built-in CSRF protection: Use Django's built-in CSRF protection to prevent CSRF attacks.
4. Use security headers: Use security headers to enhance the security of web applications.
5. Keep dependencies secure: Keep dependencies secure by regularly updating them, using a package manager, and using a virtual environment.

In conclusion, implementing advanced security practices is essential for ensuring the safety and integrity of Django applications. By implementing strategies such as XSS prevention, CSRF protection, and security headers, developers can help protect Django applications from various types of attacks. Additionally, keeping dependencies secure is essential for ensuring the overall security of web applications. By following these best practices, developers can build secure and reliable Django applications that meet the needs of their projects and applications.

In this chapter, we've explored advanced security practices for Django applications, focusing on preventing Cross-Site Scripting (XSS), securing against Cross-Site Request Forgery (CSRF) attacks, implementing security headers, and maintaining the security of dependencies. By incorporating these practices, you can significantly strengthen the security posture of your Django application.

Chapter 11: Internationalization and Localization

Ensuring that your Django applications can cater to a diverse, global audience involves addressing internationalization (i18n) and localization (l10n) challenges. In this chapter, we'll explore configuring Django for multilingual support, handling timezones and date formats, and translating content dynamically.

As web applications become more popular and reach a wider audience, it's essential to support multiple languages and locales. Django provides built-in support for internationalization and localization, making it easy to create multilingual web applications.

11.1 Configuring Django for Multilingual Support

Django's internationalization and localization features are

built on top of the GNU gettext library. The library provides a simple way to extract and translate strings in the application.

11.1.1 Setting Up Languages and Translations

Configuring Django for multilingual support involves defining the languages your application will support and setting up translations for these languages.

Example Code 1: Configuring Django for Multilingual Support

```python
# settings.py
LANGUAGE_CODE = 'en-us'
LANGUAGES = [
    ('en', _('English')),
    ('es', _('Spanish')),
    ('fr', _('French')),
    # Add more languages as needed
]


LOCALE_PATHS = [
    os.path.join(BASE_DIR, 'locale'),
]
```

To enable multilingual support in Django, follow these steps:

- Configure the available languages in the

`settings.py` file:

python
```
LANGUAGE_CODE = 'en-us'
LANGUAGES = [
    ('en', 'English'),
    ('es', 'Spanish'),
    ('fr', 'French'),
]
```

- Create translation files for each language using the
  `pybabel` tool:

##(CMD/Terminal)
```
pybabel init -i messages.pot -d
myproject/locale -l en
pybabel init -i messages.pot -d
myproject/locale -l es
pybabel init -i messages.pot -d
myproject/locale -l fr
```

- Extract strings from the application code using the
  `pybabel` tool:

##(CMD/Terminal)
```
pybabel extract -F babel.cfg -o
messages.pot myproject
```

- Translate the extracted strings using a translation
  tool, such as Poedit.

- Compile the translation files using the `pybabel` tool:


```
pybabel compile -d myproject/locale
```

Tip 1: Setting Up Languages and Translations

- Use the `LANGUAGES` setting to specify supported languages.
- Include the `LOCALE_PATHS` setting to point to the directory containing translation files.

11.1.2 Using gettext for String Translation

Django uses the gettext library for string translation. By marking strings in your code for translation, you enable Django to generate language-specific versions.

Example Code 2: Using gettext for String Translation

```python
# views.py
from django.utils.translation import gettext as _

def my_view(request):
    translated_message = _('Hello, World!')
    return render(request,
```

```python
'template.html', {'message':
translated_message})
```

Django uses the `gettext` function to extract translatable strings from the application code. The `gettext` function can be used to translate static and dynamic strings.

Here's an example of using `gettext` to translate a static string:

python
```python
from django.utils.translation import gettext as _

def my_view(request):
    message = _('Hello, world!')
    return HttpResponse(message)
```

To translate dynamic strings, use the `gettext_lazy` function:

python
```python
from django.utils.translation import gettext_lazy as _

def my_view(request):
    name = request.GET.get('name')
    message = _('Hello, %(name)s!') % {'name': name}
    return HttpResponse(message)
```

Tip 2: Using gettext for String Translation

- Wrap strings to be translated with _() or
  `gettext()` to mark them for translation.
- Use the `makemessages` management command to
  generate or update translation files.

11.2 Handling Timezones and Date Formats

Handling timezones and date formats is an essential aspect
of creating multilingual web applications. Django provides
built-in support for handling timezones and date formats.

11.2.1 Timezone-Aware Models and Views

When dealing with time-related information, it's essential to
consider timezones. Django provides tools for creating
timezone-aware models and views.

Example Code 3: Timezone-Aware Models and Views

```python
# models.py
from django.db import models


class MyModel(models.Model):
    event_time = models.DateTimeField()


# views.py
```

```python
from django.utils import timezone

def my_view(request):
    current_time = timezone.now()
    # Your view logic using timezone-aware datetime objects
```

To enable timezone support in Django, use the `USE_TZ` setting:

python
```python
USE_TZ = True
```

When `USE_TZ` is set to `True`, Django uses timezone-aware datetime objects, which automatically adjust the time based on the user's timezone.

To create timezone-aware models, use the `DateTimeField` or `DateField` fields:

python
```python
from django.db import models

class MyModel(models.Model):
    created_at = models.DateTimeField(auto_now_add=True)
    updated_at = models.DateTimeField(auto_now=True)
    published_at = models.DateTimeField()
```

To create timezone-aware views, use the `activate` function from the `django.utils.timezone` module:

python
```python
from django.utils import timezone

def my_view(request):
    timezone.activate('UTC')
    now = timezone.now()
    return HttpResponse(now)
```

Tip 3: Timezone-Aware Models and Views

- Use `DateTimeField` for storing datetime information in models.
- Always use `timezone.now()` instead of `datetime.datetime.now()` in views.

11.2.2 Customizing Date Formats

Django allows you to customize date formats for different languages and regions.

Example Code 4: Customizing Date Formats

python
```python
# settings.py
DATE_FORMAT = 'j F Y'  # Custom date format
```

Django provides built-in support for customizing date formats. To customize date formats, use the `DATE_FORMAT`, `DATETIME_FORMAT`, and `TIME_FORMAT` settings:

python
```python
DATE_FORMAT = 'j F Y'
DATETIME_FORMAT = 'D j F Y H:i:s'
TIME_FORMAT = 'H:i:s'
```

To customize date formats for a specific locale, use the `format` function from the `django.utils.formats` module:

python
```python
from django.utils.formats import localize

def my_view(request):
    date = localize(datetime.now(), format='DATE_FORMAT')
    return HttpResponse(date)
```

Tip 4: Customizing Date Formats

- Adjust `DATE_FORMAT` and other date-related settings in your `settings.py` file.
- Utilize the `{% localize %}` template tag to format dates according to the user's language preferences.

11.3 Translating Content Dynamically

Dynamically translating content is an essential aspect of creating multilingual web applications. Django provides built-in support for dynamically translating content.

11.3.1 Dynamically Changing Language Preferences

Enabling users to dynamically change their language preferences enhances the user experience.

Example Code 5: Dynamically Changing Language Preferences

```python
# views.py
from django.utils.translation import activate

def change_language(request, language_code):
    activate(language_code)
    # Your view logic
```

To dynamically change the language preference, use the `set_language` function:

```python
from django.utils.translation import
```

```
set_language

def switch_language(request):
    next_url = request.GET.get('next')
    lang_code = request.GET.get('lang')
    if lang_code:
        set_language(lang_code)
    return
HttpResponseRedirect(next_url)
```

To enable language switching in templates, use the `{% url %}` template tag:

```html
<a href="{% url 'switch_language' %}?
next={{ request.path }}
&lang=en">English</a>
<a href="{% url 'switch_language' %}?
next={{ request.path }}
&lang=es">Español</a>
<a href="{% url 'switch_language' %}?
next={{ request.path }}
&lang=fr">Français</a>
```

Tip 5: Dynamically Changing Language Preferences

- Create a language switcher view that activates the chosen language for the current user.
- Store the user's language preference in the session or user profile.

11.3.2 SEO Considerations for Multilingual Sites

When creating multilingual sites, consider search engine optimization (SEO) best practices to ensure that content is indexed correctly for different languages.

SEO is an essential aspect of creating multilingual web applications. Django provides built-in support for managing SEO in multilingual web applications.

To enable SEO support in Django, use the `sitemap` framework:

python
```python
from django.contrib import sitemaps
from django.urls import reverse


class MySitemap(sitemaps.Sitemap):
    priority = 0.5
    changefreq = 'weekly'

    def items(self):
        return MyModel.objects.all()

    def location(self, obj):
        return reverse('my_view',
args=[obj.id])
```

To customize the URLs for each language, use the `i18n_patterns` function:

python
```python
from django.urls import path, include,
```

```
i18n_patterns

urlpatterns = i18n_patterns(
    path('admin/', admin.site.urls),
    path('', include('myapp.urls')),
)
```

Examples and Tips

1. Enable multilingual support: Enable multilingual support by setting the `LANGUAGE_CODE`, `LANGUAGES`, and `LOCALE_PATHS` settings.
2. Extract translatable strings: Extract translatable strings using the `pybabel` tool.
3. Use `gettext` for string translation: Use `gettext` to translate static strings.
4. Use `gettext_lazy` for dynamic strings: Use `gettext_lazy` to translate dynamic strings.
5. Handle timezones and date formats: Handle timezones and date formats using timezone-aware datetime objects.
6. Customize date formats: Customize date formats using the `DATE_FORMAT`, `DATETIME_FORMAT`, and `TIME_FORMAT` settings.
7. Dynamically change language preferences: Dynamically change language preferences using the `set_language` function.
8. Enable SEO support: Enable SEO support using the `sitemap` framework.
9. Customize URLs for each language: Customize

URLs for each language using the
`i18n_patterns` function.

Tip 6: SEO Considerations for Multilingual Sites

- Use the `hreflang` attribute to indicate the language and regional targeting of each page.
- Create a sitemap for each language version of your site.

In conclusion, internationalization and localization are essential aspects of creating multilingual web applications. Django provides built-in support for internationalization and localization, making it easy to create multilingual web applications. By following these best practices, developers can create multilingual web applications that are accessible to a wider audience and improve the user experience.

In this chapter, we've explored advanced techniques for internationalization and localization in Django. From configuring multilingual support to handling timezones and date formats, these practices empower developers to build applications that can serve diverse global audiences seamlessly. By implementing these techniques, you can ensure that your Django applications are not only functional in different languages but also provide an optimal user experience tailored to each user's preferences.

Chapter 12: Building Extensible Django Applications

Building extensible Django applications involves designing your codebase in a way that encourages modularity, decoupling, and integration with third-party libraries. In this chapter, we'll explore writing reusable apps, using Django signals for decoupling, and integrating third-party libraries and services.

As Django applications become more complex, it's essential to design them in a way that allows for easy extensibility and maintenance. This chapter explores best practices for building extensible Django applications, including writing reusable apps, using Django signals for decoupling, and integrating third-party libraries and services.

12.1 Writing Reusable Apps

Writing reusable Django apps is the process of creating modular and self-contained components that can be easily reused in other projects. By creating reusable apps, developers can save time and effort when building new

Django applications.

12.1.1 Creating Modular Django Apps

Writing modular Django apps promotes code reuse and maintainability. A well-designed app should have clear boundaries, encapsulating its functionality.

Creating modular Django apps involves organizing the application code into smaller, self-contained components that can be easily reused in other projects. Here are some best practices for creating modular Django apps:

1. Use the `app` directory: Use the `app` directory to organize the application code.
2. Use `models.py` for database models: Use `models.py` to define the database models.
3. Use `views.py` for views: Use `views.py` to define the views.
4. Use `templates` and `static` directories: Use the `templates` and `static` directories to store the templates and static files.
5. Use `tests.py` for tests: Use `tests.py` to define the tests.

Example Code 1: Structuring a Modular Django App

```
myapp/
|-- __init__.py
```

```
|-- models.py
|-- views.py
|-- templates/
|-- static/
|-- tests/
|-- ...
```

Tip 1: Creating Modular Django Apps

- Organize code by functionalities (models, views, templates) within the app.
- Use the `tests` directory to create unit tests for your app.

12.1.2 Packaging and Distributing Apps

Packaging and distributing your Django app enable its reuse across projects. Publishing your app on platforms like PyPI allows others to install and use it easily.

Packaging and distributing Django apps makes it easy for other developers to use and integrate the app into their own projects. Here are some best practices for packaging and distributing Django apps:

1. Use a version control system: Use a version control system, such as Git, to manage the app's source code.
2. Use a package manager: Use a package manager, such as `pip`, to package and distribute the app.
3. Use a `setup.py` file: Use a `setup.py` file to define the app's metadata and dependencies.

4. Use a `README` file: Use a `README` file to provide documentation and usage instructions.
5. Use a `LICENSE` file: Use a `LICENSE` file to define the app's license.

Example Code 2: Packaging a Django App

```
myapp/
|-- MANIFEST.in
|-- setup.py
|-- myapp/
|      |-- __init__.py
|      |-- models.py
|      |-- views.py
|      |-- ...
|-- tests/
|-- ...
```

Tip 2: Packaging and Distributing Apps

- Use `setuptools` to create a `setup.py` file for packaging.
- Include a `MANIFEST.in` file to specify additional files to include in the distribution.

12.2 Using Django Signals for Decoupling

Django signals provide a way to decouple application

components and enable loose coupling between them. By using Django signals, developers can create flexible and extensible applications that are easy to maintain and update.

12.2.1 Introduction to Django Signals

Django signals allow decoupling of components by providing a mechanism for communication between different parts of the application.

Django signals are a way to send and receive notifications between application components. Django provides several built-in signals, including `pre_save`, `post_save`, `pre_delete`, and `post_delete`.

Example Code 3: Using Django Signals

```python
# signals.py
from django.db.models.signals import Signal
from django.dispatch import receiver

my_signal = Signal()

# receivers.py
from django.dispatch import receiver
from myapp.signals import my_signal

@receiver(my_signal)
def my_signal_handler(sender, **kwargs):
```

```python
    # Handle the signal
```

To use Django signals, define a signal receiver function and register it with the signal. Here's an example of using the `pre_save` signal:

python
```python
from django.db.models.signals import pre_save
from django.dispatch import receiver
from myapp.models import MyModel

@receiver(pre_save, sender=MyModel)
def my_pre_save_receiver(sender, instance, **kwargs):
    # Do something before the object is saved.
    pass
```

Tip 3: Introduction to Django Signals

- Define signals in a separate module to keep the code organized.
- Use `@receiver` decorator to connect signal handlers.

12.2.2 Real-World Examples of Signal Usage

Django signals can be applied in various scenarios, such as

updating related models or triggering actions on certain events.

Here are some real-world examples of using Django signals:

1. Auditing: Use signals to auditing changes made to database models.
2. Notifications: Use signals to send notifications to users when certain events occur.
3. Workflows: Use signals to trigger workflows based on certain events.
4. Data synchronization: Use signals to synchronize data between different models or applications.

Example Code 4: Real-World Signal Usage

```python
python
# models.py
from django.db import models
from django.db.models.signals import post_save
from django.dispatch import receiver

class UserProfile(models.Model):
    user = models.OneToOneField(User, on_delete=models.CASCADE)
    bio = models.TextField()

@receiver(post_save, sender=User)
def create_user_profile(sender,
```

```python
instance, created, **kwargs):
    if created:

UserProfile.objects.create(user=instance
)


@receiver(post_save, sender=User)
def save_user_profile(sender, instance,
**kwargs):
        instance.userprofile.save()
```

Tip 4: Real-World Examples of Signal Usage

- Use signals to automate tasks triggered by model events, such as creating related objects.
- Ensure proper testing of signal handlers to avoid unexpected behavior.

12.3 Integrating Third-Party Libraries and Services

Integrating third-party libraries and services is a common requirement for building Django applications. By integrating third-party libraries and services, developers can add new features and functionality to their applications without having to build everything from scratch.

12.3.1 Evaluating and Selecting Libraries

When selecting third-party libraries, it's essential to

evaluate them carefully to ensure that they meet the project's requirements and are compatible with the application's architecture. Here are some best practices for evaluating and selecting third-party libraries:

1. Check the documentation: Check the library's documentation to ensure that it's well-written and comprehensive.
2. Check the source code: Check the library's source code to ensure that it's well-organized and easy to understand.
3. Check the community: Check the library's community to ensure that it's active and supportive.
4. Check the compatibility: Check the library's compatibility with the application's architecture and dependencies.
5. Check the license: Check the library's license to ensure that it's compatible with the project's license.

Choosing third-party libraries involves evaluating their features, documentation, community support, and compatibility with your project.

Example Code 5: Evaluating Third-Party Libraries

```
# requirements.txt
django==3.2.5
requests==2.26.0
```

Tip 5: Evaluating and Selecting Libraries

- Check for library popularity and community activity on platforms like GitHub.
- Consider library documentation and ease of integration with Django.

12.3.2 Best Practices for Integration

Integrating third-party libraries requires adherence to best practices, including version management, security considerations, and efficient usage.

When integrating third-party libraries and services, it's essential to follow best practices to ensure that the integration is seamless and easy to maintain. Here are some best practices for integrating third-party libraries and services:

1. Use a virtual environment: Use a virtual environment to manage the library's dependencies and avoid conflicts with other libraries.
2. Use a package manager: Use a package manager, such as `pip`, to manage the library's installation and updates.
3. Use a wrapper: Use a wrapper to encapsulate the library's functionality and abstract its implementation details.
4. Use a testing strategy: Use a testing strategy to ensure that the integration is tested and validated.

5. Use a monitoring strategy: Use a monitoring strategy to ensure that the integration is monitored and maintained.

Examples and Tips

1. Create modular Django apps: Create modular Django apps by organizing the application code into smaller, self-contained components.
2. Package and distribute apps: Package and distribute Django apps using a version control system, a package manager, and a `setup.py` file.
3. Use Django signals: Use Django signals for decoupling application components and enabling loose coupling between them.
4. Evaluate and select libraries: Evaluate and select third-party libraries based on their documentation, source code, community, compatibility, and license.
5. Follow best practices for integration: Follow best practices for integrating third-party libraries and services, including using a virtual environment, a package manager, a wrapper, a testing strategy, and a monitoring strategy.

Tip 6: Best Practices for Integration

- Keep third-party libraries updated regularly to benefit from bug fixes and new features.
- Be cautious about security vulnerabilities and

subscribe to relevant security mailing lists.

In conclusion, building extensible Django applications is essential for creating applications that are easy to maintain and update. By following best practices for writing reusable apps, using Django signals for decoupling, and integrating third-party libraries and services, developers can build applications that are flexible, extensible, and easy to maintain. By incorporating these best practices into their development workflow, developers can create applications that meet the needs of their users and the requirements of their projects.

In this chapter, we've explored building extensible Django applications by writing reusable apps, using Django signals for decoupling, and integrating third-party libraries and services. By adopting these practices, you can create Django applications that are modular, maintainable, and capable of seamlessly integrating with external components, enhancing both development efficiency and application functionality.

Book Recommendations

For the mean time, I will recommend these two books for you.

- **The 1st book will teach you: 50+ Ways How to Make Money Online with Blogging, eCommerce, Affiliate Marketing, YouTube, TikTok, Facebook, Instagram, etc.**
- **While the 2nd book Focus more on Blogging, you can Pre-Order the book for now and get a better Price Deal, as the price will go up after the book is Released.**

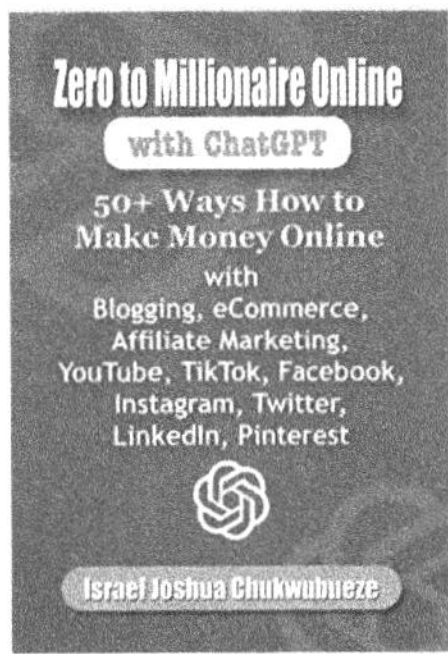

Zero to Millionaire
Online with ChatGPT:
50+ Ways How to Make
Money Online with
Blogging, eCommerce,
Affiliate Marketing,
YouTube, TikTok,
Facebook, Instagram, etc

Zero to Millionaire
Online: ChatGPT +
Blogging: Build your own
Website within 24 Hours
- Step-by-Step Guide,
How to Make Money
Online

Chapter 13: Django in a Microservices Architecture

Microservices architecture has gained popularity for building scalable and maintainable systems. In this chapter, we'll explore the fundamentals of microservices, communication between microservices, and deploying and managing microservices using technologies like Docker and Kubernetes.

In recent years, microservices have become a popular architectural pattern for building complex and scalable web applications. Django can be used in a microservices architecture, including understanding microservices, communication between microservices, and deploying and managing microservices.

13.1 Understanding Microservices

Microservices are a software development approach where an application is composed of small, independent services that communicate with each other through APIs. These services are built around specific business capabilities and can be developed, deployed, and scaled independently.

13.1.1 Advantages and Challenges

Microservices bring several advantages, such as scalability, independent deployment, and fault isolation. However, they also introduce challenges like increased complexity and potential communication overhead.

Microservices are a software development approach where an application is composed of small, independent services that communicate with each other through APIs. These services are built around specific business capabilities and can be developed, deployed, and scaled independently.

Tip 1: Advantages and Challenges of Microservices

Advantages:

- **Scalability:** Microservices can be independently scaled based on demand, allowing for more efficient resource utilization.
- **Independent Deployment:** Each microservice can be deployed independently, enabling continuous delivery.
- **Fault Isolation:** Failures in one microservice do not necessarily affect others.
- **Flexibility**: Microservices can be developed using different technologies, languages, and frameworks.
- **Resilience**: Microservices can be designed to be fault-tolerant, allowing for high availability and reliability.
- **Maintainability**: Microservices can be maintained independently, reducing the complexity of large codebases.

Challenges:

- **Increased Complexity:** Managing a larger number of services can be more complex. Microservices can be more complex to design, develop, and maintain than monolithic applications.
- **Communication Overhead:** Inter-service communication requires careful consideration.
- **Data consistency**: Microservices can have challenges with data consistency and transaction

management.

- **Testing**: Microservices can be more challenging to test due to their distributed nature.
- **Monitoring**: Microservices can be more challenging to monitor due to their distributed nature.

13.1.2 Design Principles for Microservices

Designing effective microservices involves adhering to certain principles, including service autonomy, data ownership, and well-defined APIs.

When designing microservices, it's essential to follow best practices and design principles, including:

- **Single Responsibility Principle**: Each microservice should have a single responsibility and be focused on a specific business capability.
- **API-First Design**: Microservices should be designed around APIs, allowing for loose coupling and easy integration.
- **Statelessness**: Microservices should be stateless, allowing for easy scaling and load balancing.
- **Idempotence**: Microservices should be designed to be idempotent, allowing for reliable and consistent communication.
- **Data Consistency**: Microservices should be designed to ensure data consistency and transaction management.

Tip 2: Design Principles for Microservices

Service Autonomy:

- Microservices should be autonomous and independently deployable.
- Each microservice should have its own database to avoid dependencies on other services.

Data Ownership:

- Each microservice should own its data, reducing data coupling between services.
- Data synchronization between microservices should be handled through well-defined APIs.

13.2 Communication Between Microservices

Communication between microservices is a critical aspect of a microservices architecture. There are two main approaches to communication between microservices: RESTful APIs and message queues.

13.2.1 RESTful APIs in Microservices

RESTful APIs are a common communication mechanism between microservices. Designing RESTful APIs with clear resource definitions and standard HTTP methods is crucial for effective communication.

RESTful APIs use HTTP verbs (GET, POST, PUT, DELETE) to perform CRUD operations on resources.

Advantages of RESTful APIs include:

- **Simplicity**: RESTful APIs are simple to design, develop, and maintain.
- **Interoperability**: RESTful APIs are based on open standards, allowing for easy integration with other systems.
- **Caching**: RESTful APIs can be easily cached, allowing for better performance and reduced load.

Challenges of RESTful APIs include:

- **Tight Coupling**: RESTful APIs can lead to tight coupling between microservices.
- **Latency**: RESTful APIs can have higher latency due to the overhead of HTTP requests and responses.

Example Code 1: Sample RESTful API Endpoint

```python
# views.py
from rest_framework.views import APIView
from rest_framework.response import Response
from rest_framework import status
```

```python
class OrderAPIView(APIView):
    def get(self, request, order_id):
        # Retrieve order details
        return Response(data,
status=status.HTTP_200_OK)
```

Tip 3: Designing RESTful APIs in Microservices

- Clearly define resources and endpoints to represent each microservice.
- Use standard HTTP methods for operations (GET, POST, PUT, DELETE).

13.2.2 Message Queues and Event-Driven Architecture

Message queues and event-driven architectures offer an alternative approach for communication between microservices, enabling asynchronous communication and loose coupling.

Message queues are another approach to communication between microservices. Message queues use a publish-subscribe model, where microservices can publish messages to a queue and other microservices can subscribe to those messages.

Advantages of message queues include:

- **Asynchronous**: Message queues are asynchronous,

allowing for better performance and reduced load.

- **Decoupling**: Message queues can decouple microservices, allowing for more flexible and resilient architectures.
- **Scalability**: Message queues can be scaled independently, allowing for more efficient resource utilization.

Challenges of message queues include:

- **Complexity**: Message queues can be more complex to design, develop, and maintain.
- **Monitoring**: Message queues can be more challenging to monitor due to their distributed nature.

Example Code 2: Publishing an Event to a Message Queue

```python
# publisher.py
import pika

connection = pika.BlockingConnection(pika.ConnectionParameters('localhost'))
channel = connection.channel()

channel.queue_declare(queue='order_queue')
```

```
channel.basic_publish(exchange='',
routing_key='order_queue', body='New
Order Created')
```

Tip 4: Message Queues and Event-Driven Architecture

- Use message queues like RabbitMQ or Kafka for asynchronous communication.
- Implement event-driven patterns to notify microservices of state changes.

13.3 Deploying and Managing Microservices

Deploying and managing microservices can be challenging due to their distributed nature. Containerization and orchestration are common approaches to deploying and managing microservices.

13.3.1 Containerization with Docker

Containerization with Docker simplifies the packaging and deployment of microservices, ensuring consistent environments across development, testing, and production.

Containerization is a way to package and deploy applications in a lightweight and portable way. Docker is a popular containerization platform that allows for easy deployment and management of microservices.

Advantages of containerization include:

- **Portability**: Containerization allows for easy deployment and management of microservices across different environments.
- **Isolation**: Containerization allows for isolation of microservices, reducing the risk of conflicts and dependencies.
- **Efficiency**: Containerization allows for efficient resource utilization, reducing the cost of running microservices.

Example Code 3: Dockerfile for a Django Microservice

```
Dockerfile
# Dockerfile
FROM python:3.8

WORKDIR /app

COPY requirements.txt .

RUN pip install -r requirements.txt

COPY . .

CMD ["python", "manage.py", "runserver", "0.0.0.0:8000"]
```

Tip 5: Containerization with Docker

- Define a Dockerfile for each microservice, specifying dependencies and runtime configurations.
- Utilize Docker Compose for managing multi-container applications.

13.3.2 Orchestration with Kubernetes

Kubernetes simplifies the orchestration and management of containers, providing features like automatic scaling, load balancing, and rolling updates.

Orchestration is the process of managing and scaling microservices. Kubernetes is a popular orchestration platform that allows for easy deployment and management of microservices.

Advantages of Kubernetes include:

- **Scalability**: Kubernetes allows for easy scaling of microservices, allowing for better resource utilization.
- **Resilience**: Kubernetes allows for high availability and fault tolerance, reducing the risk of downtime and failures.
- **Monitoring**: Kubernetes allows for easy monitoring and logging of microservices, allowing for better visibility and troubleshooting.

Examples and Tips

1. Understand the advantages and challenges of microservices: Understand the advantages and challenges of microservices, and design your architecture accordingly.
2. Follow design principles for microservices: Follow design principles for microservices, including the Single Responsibility Principle, API-First Design, Statelessness, Idempotence, and Data Consistency.
3. Choose the right communication approach: Choose the right communication approach between microservices, including RESTful APIs or message queues.
4. Use containerization and orchestration: Use containerization and orchestration to deploy and manage microservices, including Docker and Kubernetes.
5. Monitor and log microservices: Monitor and log microservices, allowing for better visibility and troubleshooting.

Example Code 4: Kubernetes Deployment YAML for Django Microservice

```yaml
# deployment.yaml
apiVersion: apps/v1
kind: Deployment
metadata:
```

```
      name: django-app
spec:
  replicas: 3
  selector:
    matchLabels:
      app: django-app
  template:
    metadata:
      labels:
        app: django-app
    spec:
      containers:
        - name: django-container
          image: your-django-
image:latest
          ports:
            - containerPort: 8000
```

Tip 6: Orchestration with Kubernetes

- Use Kubernetes Deployments to manage the lifecycle of microservices.
- Leverage features like auto-scaling and rolling updates for seamless operations.

In conclusion, Django can be used in a microservices architecture to build complex and scalable web applications. When designing a microservices architecture, it's essential to understand microservices, communication between microservices, and deploying and managing microservices. By following best practices and design principles, developers can build applications that are flexible, resilient, and easy to maintain. By incorporating microservices into their development workflow, developers can create applications that meet the needs of their users and the requirements of their projects.

In this chapter, we've explored the world of microservices with Django. Understanding microservices' advantages and challenges, communication mechanisms, and deployment strategies empowers developers to design scalable, maintainable, and robust systems. Whether using RESTful APIs or event-driven architectures, and deploying with Docker or Kubernetes, these techniques facilitate the successful implementation of microservices using Django.

Chapter 14: Advanced Frontend Integration

In this chapter, we'll delve into advanced frontend integration techniques to enhance the user experience of Django applications. From building Single-Page Applications (SPAs) to optimizing user experience with AJAX and incorporating WebSockets for real-time updates.

As web applications become more complex, the need for

advanced frontend integration techniques becomes increasingly important. This chapter explores advanced frontend integration techniques for Django, including building Single-Page Applications (SPAs), optimizing user experience with AJAX, and using WebSockets for real-time updates.

14.1 Building Single-Page Applications (SPAs)

Single-Page Applications (SPAs) are web applications that load a single HTML page and dynamically update the content as the user interacts with the application. SPAs can provide a more seamless user experience than traditional web applications.

14.1.1 Integrating Django with JavaScript Frameworks

Integrating Django with JavaScript frameworks like React, Vue.js, or Angular enables the development of SPAs, providing a seamless and dynamic user experience.

Integrating Django with JavaScript frameworks, such as React, Angular, or Vue.js, can be a powerful way to build SPAs. Django can act as a backend API, providing data and services to the frontend framework.

When integrating Django with a JavaScript framework, it's essential to follow best practices, including:

- **API Design**: Design a clear and consistent API that

provides the necessary data and services to the frontend framework.

- **Data Serialization**: Serialize data in a format that is easy to consume by the frontend framework, such as JSON.
- **Error Handling**: Handle errors gracefully, providing meaningful error messages and status codes.

Example Code 1: Django REST API Endpoint for a SPA

```python
# views.py
from rest_framework.views import APIView
from rest_framework.response import Response

class SPAView(APIView):
    def get(self, request):
        # Retrieve data from the backend
        data = {'message': 'Hello from the Django backend!'}
        return Response(data)
```

Tip 1: Integrating Django with JavaScript Frameworks

- Use Django REST Framework to expose APIs consumed by the SPA.
- Leverage JavaScript frameworks for dynamic content updates without full page reloads.

14.1.2 SPA Best Practices

Building SPAs involves adopting best practices to ensure maintainability, performance, and a smooth user experience.

When building SPAs, it's essential to follow best practices, including:

- **Progressive Enhancement**: Build the application with progressive enhancement techniques, allowing for graceful degradation and backward compatibility.
- **State Management**: Manage application state using a clear and consistent approach, such as using a state management library.
- **Routing**: Implement client-side routing using a clear and consistent approach, such as using a routing library.
- **Performance**: Optimize performance using techniques such as code splitting, lazy loading, and caching.

Tip 2: SPA Best Practices

State Management:

- Implement a robust state management solution provided by the chosen framework.
- Use tools like Redux or Vuex to manage complex

state logic.

Lazy Loading:

- Implement lazy loading for optimal performance, loading resources only when needed.
- Split your application into smaller modules and load them on-demand.

14.2 Optimizing User Experience with AJAX

AJAX (Asynchronous JavaScript and XML) is a technique for updating parts of a web page without requiring a full page reload. AJAX can provide a more seamless user experience than traditional page reloads.

14.2.1 Asynchronous Requests in Django

Implementing asynchronous requests with AJAX in Django allows for dynamic content updates without reloading the entire page.

Django provides support for asynchronous requests using the `XMLHttpRequest` object or the `fetch` API. Asynchronous requests can be made using the `django.views.decorators.ajax` decorator.

When making asynchronous requests in Django, it's essential to follow best practices, including:

- **Error Handling**: Handle errors gracefully, providing meaningful error messages and status codes.
- **Data Serialization**: Serialize data in a format that is easy to consume by the frontend framework, such as JSON.
- **Caching**: Cache responses when appropriate, reducing the number of requests and improving performance.

Example Code 2: Making AJAX Requests in Django Views

```javascript
// script.js
document.getElementById('load-data-btn').addEventListener('click', () => {
    fetch('/api/data/')
        .then(response => response.json())
        .then(data => {
            // Update the DOM with the retrieved data
        });
});
```

Tip 3: Asynchronous Requests in Django

- Use the Fetch API or AJAX libraries (e.g., jQuery AJAX) to make asynchronous requests.
- Ensure that your views return JSON responses for

AJAX consumption.

14.2.2 Progressive Enhancement Techniques

Applying progressive enhancement techniques ensures that your web application remains accessible and functional even when JavaScript is disabled.

Progressive enhancement techniques can be used to provide a seamless user experience for both synchronous and asynchronous requests. Progressive enhancement involves providing a basic experience for all users, and enhancing the experience for users with modern browsers and capabilities.

Examples of progressive enhancement techniques include:

- **Server-side Rendering**: Provide server-side rendering for users with older browsers, and enhance the experience for users with modern browsers using JavaScript.
- **Fallbacks**: Provide fallbacks for users with older browsers or limited capabilities, such as using a fallback image instead of a SVG.
- **Accessibility**: Provide an accessible user experience for all users, regardless of their abilities or disabilities.

Example Code 3: Graceful Degradation with Progressive Enhancement

```html
<!-- index.html -->
<button id="load-data-btn" onclick="loadData()">Load Data</button>
<noscript>This feature requires JavaScript to be enabled.</noscript>
```

Tip 4: Progressive Enhancement Techniques

- Provide alternative functionalities for users with JavaScript disabled.
- Ensure that core functionality remains accessible without relying solely on JavaScript.

14.3 Using WebSockets for Real-Time Updates

WebSockets are a protocol for real-time communication between the client and server. WebSockets can provide real-time updates and notifications to the user, improving the user experience.

14.3.1 WebSockets in Django Views

Integrating WebSockets into Django views allows for real-time communication between the server and the client.

WebSockets can be used in Django views using a

WebSocket library, such as `channels` or `django-websocket-redis`. WebSockets can be used to send real-time updates and notifications to the frontend framework.

When using WebSockets in Django views, it's essential to follow best practices, including:

- **Message Formatting**: Format messages in a clear and consistent format, such as using JSON.
- **Error Handling**: Handle errors gracefully, providing meaningful error messages and status codes.
- **Scalability**: Design for scalability, using techniques such as message queues or fan-out architectures.

Example Code 4: Django Channels Consumer for WebSocket Communication

```python
# consumers.py
import json
from channels.generic.websocket import AsyncWebsocketConsumer

class RealTimeConsumer(AsyncWebsocketConsumer):
    async def connect(self):
        await self.accept()

    async def receive(self, text_data):
```

```python
        data = json.loads(text_data)
        # Process the data and send
updates back to the client
        await
self.send(text_data=json.dumps({'message
': 'Update received'}))
```

Tip 5: WebSockets in Django Views

- Use Django Channels to handle WebSocket
  connections in Django.
- Implement asynchronous consumers to manage
  WebSocket communication.

14.3.2 Coordinating Frontend and Backend Changes

Coordinating changes between the frontend and backend in
real-time applications involves careful planning and
synchronization.

Coordinating frontend and backend changes can be
challenging when using WebSockets. It's essential to design
a clear and consistent approach for coordinating changes,
such as using an event-driven architecture.

Examples and Tips

1. Use SPAs for a more seamless user experience: Use
   SPAs to provide a more seamless user experience,
   integrating Django with JavaScript frameworks.

2. Optimize user experience with AJAX: Optimize user experience with AJAX, using asynchronous requests and progressive enhancement techniques.
3. Use WebSockets for real-time updates: Use WebSockets for real-time updates, providing real-time updates and notifications to the user.
4. Follow best practices: Follow best practices for integrating Django with JavaScript frameworks, making asynchronous requests, using WebSockets, and coordinating frontend and backend changes.
5. Test and validate: Test and validate the frontend and backend integration, ensuring that the user experience is seamless and performant.

Tip 6: Coordinating Frontend and Backend Changes

- Establish a clear communication protocol between the frontend and backend using WebSocket messages.
- Implement proper error handling and fallback mechanisms for cases where real-time updates may fail.

In conclusion, advanced frontend integration techniques, such as building Single-Page Applications (SPAs), optimizing user experience with AJAX, and using WebSockets for real-time updates, can provide a more seamless user experience for web applications. By following best practices and design principles, developers can build applications that are scalable, performant, and easy to maintain. By incorporating advanced frontend integration techniques into their development workflow, developers can create applications that meet the needs of their users and the requirements of their projects.

In this chapter, we've explored advanced frontend integration techniques for Django applications. From building SPAs and optimizing user experience with AJAX to incorporating WebSockets for real-time updates, these techniques contribute to creating dynamic and interactive web applications. By adopting best practices and understanding the nuances of each approach, developers can significantly enhance the frontend capabilities of their Django applications.

Chapter 15: Future Trends and Best Practices

As technology continually evolves, staying abreast of emerging trends and adopting best practices becomes imperative for sustainable development in the Django ecosystem.

Django is a powerful web framework that has been around for over a decade. As the web landscape continues to evolve, it's essential to stay up-to-date with emerging technologies and best practices in the Django ecosystem. In this chapter, we'll explore emerging technologies in the Django ecosystem, adopting best practices for sustainable development, and staying updated with the Django community.

15.1 Emerging Technologies in Django Ecosystem

The Django ecosystem is constantly evolving, with new technologies and tools being developed and integrated into the framework. In this section, we'll explore two emerging technologies in the Django ecosystem: GraphQL and serverless architectures.

15.1.1 GraphQL and Django

GraphQL, with its efficient and flexible querying capabilities, is gaining traction in the Django ecosystem. Integrating GraphQL with Django allows for more granular data retrieval and can enhance the performance of web applications.

GraphQL is a query language for APIs that is becoming increasingly popular in the web development community. GraphQL provides a more flexible and efficient way to retrieve and manipulate data than traditional REST APIs.

Django can be integrated with GraphQL using a library such as `graphene-django`. `graphene-django` provides a simple and intuitive way to define GraphQL schemas and resolvers for Django models.

When integrating Django with GraphQL, it's essential to follow best practices, including:

- **Schema Design**: Design a clear and consistent schema that provides the necessary data and services to the frontend framework.
- **Data Serialization**: Serialize data in a format that is easy to consume by the frontend framework, such as JSON.
- **Error Handling**: Handle errors gracefully, providing meaningful error messages and status codes.

Example Code 1: Integrating GraphQL with Django

```python
# models.py
from django.db import models

class Post(models.Model):
    title =
models.CharField(max_length=255)
    content = models.TextField()


# schema.py
import graphene
from graphene_django.types import
```

```python
DjangoObjectType
from .models import Post

class PostType(DjangoObjectType):
    class Meta:
        model = Post


class Query(graphene.ObjectType):
    all_posts = graphene.List(PostType)

    def resolve_all_posts(self, info,
**kwargs):
        return Post.objects.all()

# settings.py
INSTALLED_APPS = [
    # ...
    'graphene_django',
]
```

Tip 1: Integrating GraphQL with Django

- Use the `graphene` library to define GraphQL types and queries.
- Leverage the `graphene-django` package for seamless integration with Django models.

15.1.2 Serverless Architectures with Django

Serverless architectures, where applications are built

without managing the underlying infrastructure, offer scalability and cost-efficiency. Django applications can be adapted to serverless platforms like AWS Lambda or Google Cloud Functions.

Serverless architectures are becoming increasingly popular in the web development community. Serverless architectures provide a more scalable and cost-effective way to deploy and run web applications.

Django can be integrated with serverless architectures using a platform such as AWS Lambda. AWS Lambda allows for the deployment and execution of Django applications as serverless functions.

When integrating Django with serverless architectures, it's essential to follow best practices, including:

- **Scalability**: Design for scalability, using techniques such as message queues or fan-out architectures.
- **Performance**: Optimize performance using techniques such as caching, lazy loading, and code splitting.
- **Security**: Implement security best practices, such as using HTTPS, authentication, and authorization.

Example Code 2: Deploying a Django Function on AWS Lambda

```python
# lambda_function.py
```

```python
from django.core.wsgi import get_wsgi_application

application = get_wsgi_application()

def lambda_handler(event, context):
    return {
        'statusCode': 200,
        'body': 'Hello from Django on AWS Lambda!',
    }
```

Tip 2: Serverless Architectures with Django

- Package your Django application as a serverless function using frameworks like Zappa or Serverless Framework.
- Consider using serverless databases or storage solutions to complement serverless Django applications.

15.2 Adopting Best Practices for Sustainable Development

Sustainable development is the practice of building web applications that are scalable, maintainable, and easy to update. In this section, we'll explore two best practices for sustainable development: code reviews and collaboration, and documentation and knowledge sharing.

15.2.1 Code Reviews and Collaboration

Effective collaboration and code reviews are integral to maintaining code quality and fostering a collaborative development environment.

Code reviews and collaboration are essential best practices for sustainable development. Code reviews allow for the identification and resolution of issues early in the development process, reducing the risk of bugs and security vulnerabilities. Collaboration allows for the sharing of knowledge and expertise, improving the overall quality of the application.

Best practices for code reviews and collaboration include:

- **Tools**: Use tools such as GitHub, GitLab, or Bitbucket for code reviews and collaboration.
- **Process**: Establish a clear and consistent code review process, such as using pull requests or code review checklists.
- **Communication**: Communicate clearly and effectively, providing clear and actionable feedback.

Example Code 3: Setting Up a Code Review Workflow

1 Developers create feature branches for each task.

2   Code changes are pushed to the
     remote repository.
3   Pull Requests (PRs) are created and
     assigned for review.
4   Team members review code, leave
     comments, and suggest improvements.
5   Continuous Integration (CI) runs
     automated tests.
6   After approval, the PR is merged
     into the main branch.

Tip 3: Code Reviews and Collaboration

- Establish clear guidelines for code reviews, including coding standards and documentation requirements.
- Use collaborative tools like GitLab, GitHub, or Bitbucket for effective code collaboration.

15.2.2 Documentation and Knowledge Sharing

Maintaining comprehensive documentation ensures knowledge transfer within the development team and aids onboarding for new contributors.

Documentation and knowledge sharing are essential best practices for sustainable development. Documentation provides a clear and concise explanation of the application, reducing the risk of misunderstandings and miscommunications. Knowledge sharing allows for the transfer of expertise and best practices between team members.

Best practices for documentation and knowledge sharing include:

- **Content**: Provide clear and concise documentation, including architecture diagrams, code snippets, and user guides.
- **Format**: Use a consistent and easy-to-read format, such as Markdown or reStructuredText.
- **Accessibility**: Make documentation accessible to all team members, using tools such as a documentation portal or wiki.

Example Code 4: Documenting Django Models

```python
# models.py
from django.db import models

class Book(models.Model):
    title = models.CharField(max_length=255)
    author = models.CharField(max_length=255)
    publication_date = models.DateField()

    def __str__(self):
        return self.title
```

Tip 4: Documentation and Knowledge Sharing

- Adopt a documentation tool like Sphinx or MkDocs to create and maintain project documentation.
- Encourage the use of docstrings for individual functions and classes.

15.3 Staying Updated with the Django Community

The Django community is a vibrant and active community of developers and contributors. Staying updated with the Django community can provide valuable insights and best practices for building web applications.

15.3.1 Conferences, Meetups, and Online Communities

Engaging with the Django community through conferences, meetups, and online platforms facilitates networking, learning, and sharing experiences.

Conferences, meetups, and online communities are valuable resources for staying updated with the Django community. Conferences and meetups provide opportunities for networking and learning from other Django developers. Online communities provide a forum for discussion and collaboration.

Best practices for staying updated with the Django

community include:

- **Conferences**: Attend Django conferences, such as DjangoCon US or DjangoCon Europe.
- **Meetups**: Attend Django meetups, such as the Django Girls or DjangoBoston meetups.
- **Online Communities**: Participate in Django online communities, such as the Django subreddit or the Django Forum.

Example Code 5: Participating in a Django Meetup

1. Join a local or online Django meetup group.
2. Attend scheduled meetups to discuss topics, share experiences, and learn from others.
3. Present a lightning talk or showcase a project to contribute to the community.
4. Collaborate on open-source projects initiated within the community.

Tip 5: Conferences, Meetups, and Online Communities

- Attend DjangoCon or regional Django conferences to stay updated on the latest developments.
- Participate in online forums like the Django Forum, Reddit (r/django), and Django community Slack

channels.

15.3.2 Contributing to the Django Project

Contributing to the Django project itself not only enhances the framework but also provides invaluable learning experiences and establishes credibility within the community.

Contributing to the Django project is a valuable way to stay updated with the Django community. Contributing to the Django project allows for the sharing of expertise and best practices, improving the overall quality of the framework.

Best practices for contributing to the Django project include:

- **Issues**: Browse and contribute to Django issues, providing feedback and solutions.
- **Documentation**: Contribute to Django documentation, providing updates and improvements.
- **Code**: Contribute to Django code, providing patches and improvements.

Examples and Tips

1. Explore emerging technologies in the Django ecosystem: Explore emerging technologies in the Django ecosystem, such as GraphQL and serverless architectures.

2. Adopt best practices for sustainable development: Adopt best practices for sustainable development, such as code reviews and collaboration, and documentation and knowledge sharing.
3. Stay updated with the Django community: Stay updated with the Django community, attending conferences, meetups, and online communities, and contributing to the Django project.
4. Follow best practices for integrating Django with GraphQL: Follow best practices for integrating Django with GraphQL, such as schema design, data serialization, and error handling.
5. Follow best practices for integrating Django with serverless architectures: Follow best practices for integrating Django with serverless architectures, such as scalability, performance, and security.
6. Use tools for code reviews and collaboration: Use tools for code reviews and collaboration, such as GitHub, GitLab, or Bitbucket.
7. Use a consistent and easy-to-read format for documentation: Use a consistent and easy-to-read format for documentation, such as Markdown or reStructuredText.
8. Participate in Django online communities: Participate in Django online communities, such as the Django subreddit or the Django Forum.
9. Contribute to the Django project: Contribute to the Django project, providing feedback, documentation, and code.
10. Stay up-to-date with the latest Django releases: Stay

up-to-date with the latest Django releases, following
the official Django blog and release notes.

Example Code 6: Making a Contribution to Django

1 Fork the Django repository on
   GitHub.
2 Clone the forked repository to your
   local machine.
3 Create a feature branch for your
   contribution.
4 Make changes and push them to your
   fork.
5 Submit a Pull Request to the
   official Django repository.

Tip 6: Contributing to the Django Project

- Start with small contributions such as documentation
  updates or bug fixes.
- Follow the contribution guidelines provided by the
  Django project.

In conclusion, emerging technologies and best practices in
the Django ecosystem can provide valuable insights and
best practices for building web applications. Adopting best
practices for sustainable development, such as code reviews
and collaboration, and documentation and knowledge

sharing, can improve the overall quality and maintainability of the application. Staying updated with the Django community, attending conferences, meetups, and online communities, and contributing to the Django project, can provide valuable insights and best practices for building web applications. By incorporating these best practices and staying up-to-date with the latest trends in the Django ecosystem, developers can build applications that are scalable, maintainable, and easy to update.

In this chapter, we've explored emerging technologies in the Django ecosystem, best practices for sustainable development, and ways to stay connected with the Django community. As Django continues to evolve, adopting these practices ensures developers remain equipped with the latest tools and methodologies for building robust and scalable web applications.

Book Recommendations

The Psychology of Self-Compassion and Self-Love: Embracing Your Inner Worth

The Psychology of Emotional Intelligence: Enhancing Relationships and Self-Awareness

Book Recommendations

If you are thinking of building your YouTube Channel or TikTok Account?

- The 1st book is for you, I will teach how to use ChatGPT to come up with Video Ideas and Generate YouTube Video Scripts.
- The 2nd book is for you, I will teach how to use ChatGPT to come up with Video Ideas and Generate TikTok Video Scripts.

ChatGPT + YouTube Channel or Real Estate: How to Make $10,000-$50,000 Monthly with Your YouTube Channel and ChatGPT

Still Dismissing TikTok as Something for the kids? : Short-form video content created by ChatGPT is exploding right now!